SETH
CREATIVE EXPRESSION

DALE LANDRY

EDITED BY: RICHARD GLAESSER

Editors: Erna Glaesser, Debra Jones,
Christine Zeldin & Richard LeBlanc

Cover illustration & design: Jock MacRae

3rd
EYE
PUBLISHING

Copyright Page

3rd Eye Publishing
c/o Hushion House Publishing Limited
36 Northline Road
Toronto, Ontario
Canada M4B 3E2

Seth: Creative Expression
ISBN 0-9684678-0-6
Dale Landry

Editors: Erna Glaesser, Richard Glaesser, Deborah Jones, Richard Leblanc and Christine Zeldin

Cover illustration and design: Jock McRae

Quantity discounted orders are available for groups. Please make enquiries by writing directly to the publisher.

Printing history
Printed in Canada

DEDICATION

I am dedicating this book to my brothers and sisters who may be at a distance but are never far from my heart.

Shirley Anne Hannah
David Paul Landry
Joan Marie Kane
Bernard James Landry
John Patrick Landry
William Giles Landry
Sarah Elizabeth Landry
Francis Eleanor Marie Landry
Monica Rosalie Landry

ABOUT THE AUTHOR

Since 1983, Dale Landry has developed his visionary gift as a trance channeller. Graduating with a Bachelor of Arts in Psychology, Dale works with many individuals helping them in their spiritual quest for personal growth and development.

INTRODUCTION

Working on this book and channelling the soul of Seth was a true labour of love. It is difficult, however, to clearly explain what channelling is all about. Simply put, channelling, also known as trance channelling, occurs when a living person descends into a trance-like state and allows a soul from spirit (i.e., the metaphysical realm) to enter his or her body to deliver information. The physical act of channelling provides meaning and reason for why we inhabit the earth. It is often assumed that channelling and psychic phenomena have little importance in our purpose for existing. However, to look more closely at the issue, we did not originate as just one molecule but as hundreds of thousands of molecules, each with its own purpose.

Once I decided to write *Seth: Creative Expression*, I felt that it was important to ask Christine Zeldin, a very dedicated student from one of my classes, to sit with me while I channelled the soul of Seth who dictated the information for this book. When one channels a soul from spirit, this person requires at least one other person to sit with him or her, to utilize that other person's energy, and to assist the channeller to hold within their body the soul from spirit.

Our channelling sessions were held in the front room of my home, with Christine sitting directly across from myself. Christine assisted me to record the information I was channelling and transcribed the tape recorded sessions at her home. The transcribed sessions were then proofread and edited by four individuals, Erna Glaesser, Richard Glaesser, Richard Leblanc and Deborah Jones.

Seth: Creative Expression is written in a conversational format and you must take this into account when you read it. In each session, Seth speaks directly to you, the reader, but there are other times when he converses briefly with Christine to determine her feelings about the information being discussed. Furthermore, Seth's information contains many ideas and often jumps from thought to thought. But each thought has a significant message and you must 'think' about how it pertains to your life.

Similar to the structure of my last book, *The Voices of Spirit: Predictions for the New Millennium, Seth: Creative Expression* was developed over a number of one- to two-hour sessions beginning from May 1998 to mid-June 1998; each session is identified accordingly. However, what is different from the last book is that Christine shares her perceptions of each session throughout the development of this book, including her emotional experiences and personal growth. The reason for providing this additional information is to give you a sense of what to expect. The information provided by Christine has been set in italics to help you distinguish between Seth's information and Christine's commentary.

In addition, the reason why I chose the soul of Seth was due to my respect for the now deceased channeller Jane Roberts. Seth was the main teacher or personal guide to Jane Roberts. (It is believed that each living person has at least one soul from spirit which acts as his or her teacher, spirit or personal guide.) Jane Roberts wrote a number of books in which she channelled the entity of Seth alongside her husband Robert Butts. Like Christine with myself, Robert sat with Jane during each session to write her books. For *Seth: Creative Expression*, the soul of Seth has come to me strictly as an inspirational soul and not as a personal guide or teacher. My personal guide is Dr. Smithson who works with me each day on a variety of personal growth and spiritual issues. With some personal guides, their origin at the time they inhabited the earth is unknown.

The souls I have channelled to write my books including, Nostradamus for *The Voices of Spirit*, the soul of Seth for *Seth: Creative Expression*, and Jesus Christ for *The Christ Spirit*, should not be confused with the relationship I have with my personal guide, Dr. Smithson. I do not feel that I am 'special' because I can channel Nostradamus, Seth and Christ. Like every living person, all souls from spirit have experienced our physical reality (our physical world) and know well the difficulties and pain each living person encounters.

Do not judge too quickly the material you read in *Seth: Creative Expression*, but take from it the ideas which may resolve difficult questions or provide direction to problematic issues. Channelling a spirit is a tool to gain knowledge, wisdom and insight just like the violin is an instrument to produce beautiful, passionate music. In this regard, whatever tools or instruments you use to enhance your personal growth can be either beneficial or detrimental, depending on how you use them.

In closing, I would like to thank the many people who have made *Seth: Creative Expression* a positive experience. To mention each person's name is not possible, but their assistance reflects the notion that you can draw on the support of those close around you to achieve your goals and purpose. Friends, relatives, acquaintances and business associates can help you make your dreams come true; these people are not as far away as you may think.

Dale Landry

A WORD FROM CHRISTINE ZELDIN

(Assistant to Dale Landry during the Seth sessions)

*T*o explain my role in Dale's book, Seth: Creative Expression, *is relatively easy. One week before starting the book, Dale approached me and asked if I would be interested in assisting him on this project. My role would involve sitting and transcribing each tape recorded session with Dale while he channelled Seth's information. Dale mentioned that dictating the book would take about two hours a night, four nights a week, for approximately two months.*

It is difficult to put into words my surprise and excitement when I was asked to work on this project. I felt a rush of energy that had me on a spiritual high for days, if not weeks. As Dale began channelling the sessions, I had a seemingly endless stream of thoughts, energy and excitement that pervaded my day-to-day existence. Seth's impact on me as he came through Dale to speak was unlike anything I had ever experienced before.

Seth requested I make a series of notes, mainly at the beginning and at the end of each session. These notes explain my thoughts and observations before, during and after the sessions.

I often felt that my notes were too general, somewhat inadequate and irrelevant. But as Seth stated later in the book, my thoughts and observations could be crucial to you, the reader. They should prompt you to recognize the importance of your life and the possibility of what you could obtain by reaching deep within your thoughts to see beyond the mundane.

When I completed the initial draft of my notes for each session, I discovered many more details that needed to be revised in order to complete the book. Richard Glaesser, one of the book's editors, was ruthless in his desire for perfection and I was quite fearful of being "wiped clean of ever having existed in the sessions"—I think that's how it's put. I certainly didn't know that 'perfection' and the pursuit of godliness had such a high price tag. But when all is said and done, I am satisfied that my work with Dale and Seth was perfection of mental, emotional, physical and spiritual proportions.

I only hope that as you read these pages you experience even a small part of what I did. If anything, I know it will captivate you in ways you will not expect.

Christine Zeldin

UNDERSTANDING
CREATIVE EXPRESSION

Saturday, May 2, 1998 - Dale and I had agreed to meet at twelve noon to begin the dictation on Seth's book. I arrived on time, but had apparently missed Dale's call asking that our session be postponed to 12:30 in the afternoon. On the spur of the moment, a client of Dale's requested a 'channelling' appointment with him, and this had delayed our first session. However, it worked out in the end because Dale's roommates Laura and Sarah (also his sister), both kept me company.

There was a constant flurry of friends coming and going from Dale's house; a sort of 'open door' policy. I sometimes wondered how I would handle this spontaneity under similar circumstances. I had become accustomed to spending a great deal of time on my own.

Before starting the first session, I had a memory from my youth—a feeling of wanting to be invisible—and wondered why this feeling was coming out at this moment.

Dale was ready to begin channelling.

Children from an early age are able to undertake a variety of creative projects. At the age of five, or even younger, a child's mind is capable of expressing, reflecting and manipulating its environment. It is also the child's mind that has the unique capacity of initiating, creating understanding and adopting its entire surroundings.

From the age of four and into later years, a child becomes aware that there are limitations and boundaries to its environment. By the age of nine, a child is well acquainted with the basic elements that will sustain its creativity throughout the rest of his or her life. Individuals who were not introduced to their creativity by the time they reached the age of nine may pursue their artistic talents later on in life. And, if both genders by the age of fifty have never consciously been exposed to their creativity, they may go back to their younger years and express their creative passions once again.

To understand the true origin of your creativity, you need to know where you are coming from. You have to explore your childhood years, the environment you lived in as well as the surroundings that allowed you to express your creative freedom until you were nine years old. However, to take in the total picture of your creative talents, it is of equal importance for you to understand where your parents spent their younger years, as well as to explore the creative freedom they had until they reached the age of nine.

Financial and material restrictions in life do not hinder creative endeavours, only physical abuse has the power of destroying creative growth and maturity. Therefore, individuals who were victims of physical abuse, may later on become authorities in the field of probing and manipulating their lives, and, in their minds, they employ these skills only to escape from further physical attacks. Often times, to cope with the abuse, young people manipulate their environment and develop an understanding for motives and actions, to protect them from further persecution.

At the age of four, a lonely child may create imaginary siblings and friends only to use them to express a desire for being needed. A child, even at the tender age of four, can understand loneliness. However, adults are not always aware of a child's lonely feelings, and the notion exists that children are too young to understand their feelings or their environment. Yet, young children do understand their environment, are vulnerable and open to their surroundings, and to everyone they connect with.

To gain a better understanding of your creative needs, revert back to your youth and search the avenues you opened to uncover your creative desires. If, at the age of four, you were allowed to express an abundance of creative play and laughter, then, later on in life you may choose the same means to express your creativity. But, if in your childhood you created only images and physical thoughts then, as you grow older, you probably will continue on the path of these explicit desires.

Children at four years old who are able to display their superiority in many areas of their activities, do not have the ability to comprehend what life may have in store for them in later years. Yet, even though they may differ in their natural abilities, most children are remarkably aware of what their parents expect of them. For example, if a mother's ambition is for her child to be a great pianist, then the little boy or girl may act out her desire and invent a make-believe piano to become the great pianist she always dreamed of having. But, later on in life that little imaginary "adventure" may never be remembered.

In trying to gain a deeper understanding of yourself, you must attempt to analyze your mother's emotional state at the time of your birth. If your mother, during that time, felt trapped and deprived of her creative freedom then, you too, may be lacking in your creative freedom. But, if your mother was in a creative frame of mind and expressed enjoyment in having her home and career, then you grew up in a surrounding that allowed you to express your creativity at anytime throughout your life.

In North America, for example, society does not consider creativity to be of real importance, and, therefore, creativity is not valued as an essential part of personal or economic survival. In reality, however, society cries out for creative expression—yet, creative expression must not be confused with emotional expression. It is important to observe that emotions are distinct and must not be considered creative even though they can be developed to serve a creative purpose. It is also important to understand that emotional expression is one thing and creative expression another.

North American society fails to encourage children or young people to pursue their creativity. It fails to motivate children and young people to actively express their creativity through painting, singing, playing musical instruments, drawing or even inventing something. Therefore, the result is that many of these children and young people expect to be entertained instead of taking advantage of their creativity by entertaining themselves.

Art is a creative expression; it is an expression that may lead to a better understanding of yourself. For example, if you are going to paint a picture, consider it a reflection of yourself. Therefore, it is not important how the picture is viewed by others since these individuals only express an opinion and do not interpret the true value of the picture. However, at times, society does put a value on things that are personal, but again, these are opinions, and, ironically, opinions are only speculations and are of no value at all.

If your creative nature has been stifled but you wish to explore it further, you may experience a sense of fulfilment in so doing, and not only because of the creative process involved, but because you have been starving until now to express yourself creatively.

If you do spend most of your adult years locked into a routine that allows for nothing else but work, homelife and caring for a family, then there is no time left to unlock your creativity. And, if you do continue on a path of creative unfulfillment, by the time you are fifty years old you will find life less than rewarding. You may continue searching for creative outlets through friends, family or other people who bring meaning into your life, but if your creative needs are not met, the result will always be the same—a life that is boring and unfulfilling. But remember, you are not alone in this. Many individuals who appear 'happy' hunger for a sense of direction and purpose in life, and many never find it.

Throughout your growing years you were taught to protect your emotions, often at the expense of pleasing others. It is not a fulfilling life to deny your creativity and emotions only to satisfy others. Therefore, to find creative fulfilment in your life, you must pursue other avenues to express your creativity and assure yourself of the creative freedom that you so richly deserve.

To put forward an example: community theatre for a fifty-year old is a great avenue for acting out youthful desires. It is not only the process of acting that is so inspiring, but it is also the desire and the need for self expression that is fulfilled, as well as the feeling of being creatively connected with the inner self. Those individuals who do undertake this process are well rewarded for their accomplishments, however, those who scorn such projects, restrict themselves in ways that make their lives less than meaningful. Therefore, if you are trying to attain your life's purpose, you must not fear the struggle of fulfilling your desire to make your life complete.

Without expressing your emotions, it is difficult to find the outlet for creative expression, for one complements the other. Yet, emotional feelings are frowned upon. Society even isolates men and women who express their feelings, and not because these individuals are weak, but because they are different.

The new millennium will be a time of communication and expression. There will be constant change as the world learns to adapt to this new period, and the changes will take place in many ways. For instance, one day you may feel secure with your life, and the very next you may have to deal with the chaos. However, individuals who do adapt quickly will function well in their new environment, and creative expression will be one way of dealing with these changes. To challenge the environment will have almost no effect; you cannot challenge what you cannot control, nor can you prepare for it. You can build a home with a firm foundation to prepare for possible earthquakes, but will this home withstand the floods? There will be uncertainty in the age of Aquarius, since this period in the new millennium will be a period of constant fluctuations. The age of Aquarius will be about change, self-expression and determining your destiny. You can achieve a fulfilling and creative life in those times through self-expression and by defining specific goals.

In summarizing this session, it is important to understand that material wealth does not always indicate success in life. It is the creative expression that leads to self-awareness, to a sense of accomplishment and self-worth; material success without creative expression leads to a life that is only a mere existence. However, as you are reading through this book, your own creativity will emerge and you will learn to understand that only creativity can bring purpose and peace to your life.

I sat through our first session so quietly and so completely absorbed by Seth's dictation that, throughout the hour we spent together, it was as if he was speaking only to me.

Seth had triggered memories of my childhood, my parents, my friends, the fun times, but also the creative expression that was stifled in my youth. What bothered me the most was trying to recall my primary years, the years before age five, where I really had no memory at all.

While sitting in the session, I desired so strongly to understand all of what Seth was saying. Yet, funny as it seems, I knew instinctively that there were so many deeper levels of thought and meaning to what he was saying and that it would take me a great deal of time and effort to grasp the bits and pieces of it.

I knew that by sitting through and transcribing each of these sessions, doors would begin to open that not even I could see.

When we stopped recording, Seth continued speaking to me. It was a light conversation and clearly Seth was more relaxed than I was. Following our discussion, Seth said his good-byes and wished me well.

When Dale came out of trance, we elaborated on the information being delivered. The insight concerning how much of our lives are formulated from childhood is a familiar one, but I hadn't thoroughly pursued it to the degree that it continually impacted our lives. As I was sitting and talking to Dale, I was totally captivated, and in awe of all that he knew on this subject as well as what he experienced in trance. I wondered what it would be like if I also channelled, but I didn't dare voice my thoughts for fear that I might hear myself.

Since Dale and I both had a full evening ahead, we said good-bye to each other and shared our excitement for what was to follow.

THE LANGUAGE OF ART

*M*onday, May 4, 1998 - *The front door to Dale's house was closed but I knew it was unlocked. It wasn't necessary to ring the door bell. It was understood that when you were expected, the door would be open and you could walk right in.*

A CD was playing as I walked in, and over the music I announced my arrival. It was no use though; I knew no one would hear my voice. In working with Dale and doing personal growth classes with him, I got to know him quite well. I realized quickly that he was not meticulous and rarely punctual. But his gifts, the channelling and his creativity, made up for his faults in my eyes.

I made my way to the kitchen in the back of the house and met Laura, his roommate, who was making dinner for herself. We talked a bit about our day and then Laura said that Dale was downstairs in the basement. I caught up with him as he finished writing some notes. He looked up when I came in and said he was ready to start our next session.

We spoke briefly about the similarity of our day's events. This, in part, we agreed was a cause and effect of the channelling sessions.

I found it difficult to contain my enthusiasm that I was involved in the creation of this book.

We finally sat down in the 'channelling' room, and Dale began the session.

7

If someone instructed you to draw a picture of the past five years of your life, you would be amazed to discover how eventful and pivotal your life has been, and how much you have progressed and achieved during that time. But there are still many people who are searching for answers to questions like "Why am I here?", "What do I need to accomplish in my life?" and "What will the future hold for me?" It is important to understand that these questions can be answered through artistic expression.

Some day the time will come, and we will add another language to our languages that already exist. If you could draw your life in pictures from the age of three to eighteen, you would have learned to express yourself through another language—the Language of Art. Perhaps, in future, people who express themselves artistically will ask each other: "Do you speak Art?" and most will understand the meaning of this question and answer: "Yes, I do."

There are so many areas in our lives that remain a mystery. People live in the present, yet they question their future. And some reject the present since their lives at that moment might be too painful to bear. The Language of Art allows people to draw a picture of their lives, not literally, but in their minds, and for you, what would it reveal? Would it be painful and tragic, or would it unmask a 'happier' you? What would your present circumstances uncover? Would it reveal love, hate, rejection, despair, compassion or insight?

People have strong beliefs about what the quality of their lives should be, instead of facing reality and accepting life as it is. If, for instance, you were to challenge your life through artistic expression, would you express yourself in ways other than only artistic endeavours? It is unfortunate that in our society men are conditioned to believe that to show their masculinity they must be powerful and controlling. Yet, these very same men are lacking the fundamental skills to understand their own emotions. Their personal failure to recognize the value of their emotions leaves them in a state of denying themselves and their most profound experiences.

Women, in turn, are taught to shelter their voice but are encouraged to feel and express their emotions. Unfortunately, they are judged as being inadequate for carrying out what they have been taught to do.

Through your inner voice and creative nature, you can find strength, balance, harmony and individuality. You can enjoy a future that includes everyone, not just a few. But to encompass everyone, each and every individual must work together to find peace and harmony.

The United States and other countries have made great strides in the field of communication, and the approaching millennium will be a time of creating many new avenues of communication and technology. This will enable people to speak to each other through thoughts without using words. But not all emotions can be communicated through thoughts; at times, only the intent of an emotion can be expressed, and anger is one of these emotions. But even then, there will be many individuals who will feel hindered to express themselves emotionally, intuitively and spiritually.

The period between the year 2000 and 2010 will hold many new changes and a great deal of movement. There also exists a common belief that only those who can keep pace with the newest inventions and communication modes will survive. But to take a closer look at business today, it is evident that most individuals will eventually perish, and many will start over again with a fresh approach to commerce and finance. Tapping into your own creative resources, going to school or teaching yourself the craft of drawing, singing, or a variety of other skills, may symbolize only an elementary venture, but the true expression of art will not be that easy. Teach the eye to see, the ear to hear—simply, learn the Language of Art. The Language of Art is reinvented, built upon, reestablished, reorganized, rethought and presented from a different perspective later on in life. And remember, the Language of Art has to be developed and mastered while you are still young.

You may question whether my theory of Art is important. By 2005, there will be a development towards different forms of art. For instance, the sculpting of a totem pole will be interpreted as one form of art. Now, I pose the question, is this language or the development of this artform dead? What did it represent to the native culture? By destroying the natives, do we destroy a part of ourselves, a part of our heritage, or a part of our language? Society has shown little regard for the native art, an art which has demonstrated only adoration and respect for nature. Over the years, there is much the native culture has endured, and much more society could have learned from it.

Picture a woman living in New York city. She lives alone in a small apartment, has no friends, and the only personal contact she has is with people she meets at her job. Her weekends are empty and lonely, and she has nothing in life but her work; she lives a life of despair. Such a picture would move anyone to question the values a society has created for itself over the past twenty to thirty years.

But now, let us focus on a different picture. The very same woman is going to her place of employment, is enthusiastically discussing her dedication to art, her various forms of communication, and, most of all, she is happy to be able to inspire others to follow her devotion to art. This woman now has a goal, a purpose in life, and through her art she is creating a community that is drawn together and not split apart.

If each person was treated equally, how diverse and successful a society we would have. To some, food without spices is sinful, but if spices are added—a mixture of many different cultures—it would add zest, it would add life.

As Seth interpreted our world, images flowed through my mind of the many scenarios he presented, meshed with my own flashbacks of how I related to the world around me. How many times have I tried to voice my opinions over the years, feeling inadequate for doing so, always believing that someone else had something better to say. I still felt somewhat unresolved in the emotional turmoil that was beginning to surface.

After the tape finished, Seth spoke directly to me and provided further insight which he did not allow me to record. He explained that someday I would understand why. I had a sense it had something to do with Dale, however, I wasn't sure.

At this point, I could hear people in the kitchen laughing and talking. They were obviously preparing dinner. The clatter of pots and pans, running water, and the aroma of frying onions told me something good was happening.

As the session was coming to a close, Seth and I continued talking. Or, more to the point, Seth spoke to me. I listened and said little; a silence I continued to maintain in his presence.

When Seth and I finished, Dale came out of trance quite quickly and was still stimulated from the session. This sparked another conversation between us.

Dale invited me to stay for dinner and as we walked through the house to the kitchen, Sarah and Corinne, another friend of ours, had dinner well underway. Dale helped with dinner and soon we were all eating at the table. The atmosphere was very relaxing and I thoroughly enjoyed our meal together.

COMMUNICATION

Tuesday, May 5, 1998 - The stream of warm weather we were experiencing was refreshing. It made travelling to Dale's home very pleasant. Upon arriving this evening, there was only Laura at home. Rick's bike had broken down and Dale headed out to help him (Rick was Dale's other roommate). Laura and I kept each other company until they returned. Laura works in the film industry and there was always something of interest to talk about with her. It wasn't long until Dale and Rick returned and we all took a moment to sit outside on the front porch, enjoy the fresh air and have a cup of coffee before beginning our session.

Men and women question their existence often—What is my purpose in life? Is this the only reality? Is there a God? At the beginning of time—or what you see as time—we could assume that human existence was either incredibly harsh or a tropical paradise, a 'Garden of Eden' of sorts. I prefer to think of the latter, for today many would find it difficult to believe that such a paradise ever existed.

In the beginning, the language used to communicate was a 'knowingness'. It was a form of communication that allowed the thoughts and desires of one person to be transmitted to another without words. This was not a form of telepathy. It was beyond telepathy—it was knowingness. However, as people started to move further apart physically, the 'knowingness' as a form of communication became more difficult and much different. As time passed and communication became more archaic, people communicated through telepathy. And following telepathy, it was not the voice that came into the foreground as most people would assume, but a type of sign language.

From all indications here, the physical world began millions of years ago, but the earlier forms of communication have not been lost. The ability to make use of them is within the grasp of all living individuals. People of superior intelligence can communicate through knowingness, others may resort to telepathy. However, many fear utilizing this ability of 'knowingness' because they question whether it would label them as outcasts in society's eyes. The most recent form of communication is speech, and mingled with speech is emotional expression. This form of expression, however, can be attributed more to the characteristics of sign language. In sign language, there is an element of deep feeling expressed through physical emotions. Finally, there is artistic communication which is, as you will see, a language unto its own.

I wish to address the inception of humankind. To inhabit the earth, the metaphysical soul, referred to as spirit, had to start at a very high frequency and gradually lowered its frequency until it could inhabit the earth. This frequency is also referred to as a vibration or an energy. Each soul on both the physical and metaphysical planes has a frequency. Souls in the metaphysical do not communicate through speech, but through an intuitive connection, a 'knowingness'. This is why knowingness was the first form of communication when humankind first inhabited the earth. Souls in spirit still communicate through a form of knowingness. However, there are many different frequencies in spirit and over time on your physical plane people will become more aware of them.

As the age of Aquarius flourishes, people will start to analyze the different areas of their souls that carry the many artistic expressions which have evolved throughout the past lives of each individual. I view each life as an artistic expression, and if you have travelled through 10,000 or 20,000 lives, you can envision the incredible collage of colourful images you have had to deal with.

Take a closer look at your artistic expressions and you will begin the process of questioning your life purpose. You travel through many different lifetimes on this physical plane simply learning to survive. Through each life, as a part of this survival process, you have also developed an increasingly stronger awareness of your purpose and reason for existing in this physical reality. When your soul returns to spirit, it uses the skills it has learned over its many lifetimes to create alternate realities. Alternate realities are alternate purposes beyond your physical plane. To add clarity to this idea, picture yourself as a child in spirit. Because you exist in spirit, you can never grow old. You are continually expanding your knowledge, your insight, and you are working to find your purpose. Your purpose may be to reincarnate into other realities and other worlds, metaphysical or otherwise.

Imagine an alternate reality in which the only existence is pure thought. Since you have a physical body in this vibration, you might ask: "What would be the purpose of existing as pure thought?" In answer to your question, I suggest, "Are your loved ones in spirit not only pure thought with no physical vibration?" Souls who exist in the metaphysical are there for a purpose. Your life does not end when the physical body passes away.

Society's ritual for dealing with death goes back to the beginning of time. At that time, it was believed that for a soul to pass into spirit it had to be blessed by religious and ceremonial customs.

People constantly question the meaning of their existence, but your purpose lies within you. There are many reasons why you have lived through other lifetimes, including this one. Look underneath the surface to discover the contents. Through greater thought and exploration, you will discover a multitude of lives, each having provided you with unique characteristics, gifts and assets which add purpose to this life.

Through the age of Aquarius, you will escape the shackles of your flesh. You will metamorphasize like a caterpillar and discover the wonderful array of colours and images that you are, each a reflection of your potential and purpose.

Communication is such a big part of our lives and I found tonight's session very fascinating. I pondered Seth's words and knew I would do better in a world of 'knowingness' and 'telepathy'. I am the type of person who expects others to know what I am thinking. To verbally express my wants, desires and true thoughts does not come easily. My thoughts are always crystal clear in my mind but, somewhere in the translation, I can not properly articulate the words. I am conscious of this limitation and have problems putting all of my thoughts into words. Even so, I sill don't feel I always get my point across clearly.

For the first time tonight I discovered the root of my uneasiness. After we finished, Seth asked me to begin writing down my thoughts after each session to include in the book. I was caught off guard and didn't know how to reply. Seth assured me all would be well and encouraged me to start writing. The mere thought of writing for other people was frightening. However, as my mind began to process the idea, I knew I couldn't pass up the chance to work with Seth. Initially, my involvement was to simply transcribe the notes, but in the flash of a moment, I had reached an exciting turn of events. When Dale came out of trance he also liked the idea. But, it wasn't until then that I sensed he already knew I would be doing this.

One other thought I had, consistent from session to session, was Dale's ability to set aside his beliefs, and allow the soul of Seth to come through to give his interpretations and ideas. I often wondered if Dale knew how important Seth's material was, and whether or not he could see the relevance of Seth's information to his own life. So many thoughts, so little time. Ha, ha.

I again received another invitation to stay for dinner.

$\mathscr{S}$ESSION 4A

CAPTIVITY

*W*ednesday, May 6, 1998 - Our sessions to date had rarely started on time, and I always took the opportunity to socialize with whomever was in the house. Tonight, I met Sarah and we decided to go across the street for a cup of coffee. Once again, I found myself outside on the porch enjoying some light conversation with Sarah before Dale arrived.

In doing these sessions, one thing I noticed was that, with each passing day, things at work and at home appeared to become much simpler. The complexities and confusion of life was always so constant before these sessions began, and now I was enjoying the clarity that was seemingly more present.

Clearly, channelling with Dale and Seth was having a strong impact upon me. I don't know how I had lived before, so distant, and in such an archaic manner.

Finally, Dale arrived and we began the session.

There are ways to alleviate the struggles that persist when you feel mentally imprisoned. Most people suffer in their lives from a fear of mental captivity, and these phobias may have been carried over from past lives, and now, are passed down through artistic incarnations.

For instance, if you had been accidentally shot in your past life, it would justify the unexplained fear in your present life that you have of being shot or killed. This irrational fear may even intensify when you find yourself among strangers. It is also conceivable that you might have an inherent fear of dying unexpectedly, and this mental bondage may have been carried over from a previous life. You may not be aware that your soul is plagued by fears from past lives, and, therefore, you may not be ready to deal with them in your present life. Yet, your soul may delegate these fears to other lives, for instance, to five consecutive lifetimes in the future, in order to deal with them more effectively.

It is important to understand that, in today's society, the way out of mental restraints is to look inwardly, but it would be ineffective if you did not know what you have look for.

To understand your inner being, try to understand your fears, as well as your character, and ask yourself the questions which go to the heart of your inner core. Eventually, the more questions you ask yourself, the more thought provoking the process will be, and the more understanding you will gain of your inner self. Imagine yourself as a puzzle consisting of about 5,000 pieces. By the time you are 20 years old, you may have used only 100 pieces. Clearly, that should tell you that more work has to be done for personal understanding. Remember, however, gaining an understanding of your 'self' can begin at any time in your life. Keep in mind that if your parents were eager to gain a deeper understanding of their inner selves, then you, too, would start the search for your personal understanding at an earlier age.

People are not punished for not completing the puzzle. Instead, they will simply have an empty board, with many unsolved puzzle pieces, and the work to understand the 'self' will pile up. This unfinished work will be added to the karma and the lessons you have neglected to learn at that moment. It may carry over into another lifetime, or, perhaps, you may transfer these unresolved issues into illness or mental stress.

In conclusion, do not regard this session as a picture of doom and gloom, but rather appreciate the reasons why you are in this world, and why you pass over into spirit. Also, understand that living a life of ignorance does not lead to bliss, but rather, it leads to a life of constant pain for which there is a high price to pay.

Over the past several years, I had come to know more and more about myself, yet realized there was always something new to learn in one's life. And as I continued to sit in these sessions I became more aware of how little I knew, and how long the road was to travel.

I was especially interested in the effects of karma. My personal growth was focused on my emotions, my character, what I reflected and projected on to others, and my repetitive patterns. I paid little attention to karma. Even though, at one time, it was suggested that I pay more attention to it since it played an integral role in my personal development. But, when I focus on one part of learning the 'self', it is easy to ignore other outside thoughts.

Although this chapter was over, Seth decided he would continue dictating into the next one.

DENIAL

Wednesday, May 6, 1998 - (continued)

Certain aspects of life take a long time to recognize such as your emotional, physical, mental and spiritual well-being. Sometimes, those who have experienced a traumatic childhood remember little about the difficult times, and only live in the present and the future. For instance, a right-handed person may sever his left hand thinking the left hand is unimportant. However, even if he used his right hand for most of his daily tasks, every so often he will want to use the left. And each time he will be reminded of his thoughts that he believed his left hand was unimportant. So, if you emotionally sever yourself from your experiences in youth, you may think your younger years were unimportant, and decide not to look back and acknowledge what has transpired. This is a part of 'denial'.

Denial allows you to pretend there is little pain in your life, yet the pain is quite real, just as love and compassion are real. It is also part of choosing to acknowledge only certain parts of your youth, and eliminating others which you believe your memory has forgotten.

The reason why memories are forgotten is because the mind and body sever the difficult times to help you move forward through life, without being held back by pain and difficulties. Nevertheless, just as pain from one lifetime can spill over into the next, these painful, yet forgotten experiences in your present life, remain. At some point, you must deal with the remnants of your past lives, as you must deal with the pain of the present.

People believe they can escape life's responsibilities. But, eventually, either in this life or another, they will find themselves unable to run and must take responsibility for what they have been avoiding. Many people, unless backed against the wall, will not accept certain responsibilities that will allow them to progress forward and clear their karmic debt.

Often, the reason why relationships fail is because people will not accept emotional responsibility for themselves. Ultimately, it is impossible for the other party in the relationship to take on their partner's emotional baggage. Love can only survive when you are willing to accept your emotions, your failings and your disappointments. The process of personal growth may continue until the age of 65. To coin a phrase, "good things come to those who wait," and you will only stand to gain from the work you do to understand your 'self'. I have discussed the ideas of captivity and denial to give you answers and to help you to develop a new understanding of your inner core.

I found it interesting that Seth would bring up the 'missing childhood years'. It so closely resembled my life, and the years I felt that were missing. There was a part of me that was very reluctant to hear what he had to say during these sessions. Yet, I knew that if I wanted to grow and develop, it was important to look deep within, regardless of my fears.

I did not believe deep in my heart that my youth was really that difficult. And, still, a part of me wanted to bypass this session.

How was it that Seth could so clearly describe what so many people, such as myself, had experienced by denying their youth and its pain? I had always seen myself as average, unattractive, with not much opportunity in life. But, the message was clear. "Get off your ass, Christine, and do some work."

'Mohammed' stood before the mountain as my thoughts roamed about the unforgotten years.

DEGREES OF SEPARATION

Thursday, May 7, 1998 - At one point today at work, I allowed myself to drift off and observe my co-workers. In particular, I took note of the people in my office who shared mutual interests, and the personal attributes of each individual. What was interesting about this experience was that I never scrutinized people before so intensely.

I still needed to earn a living so these moments of observation were short lived. Invariably, I resumed my work, but still allowed myself to occasionally watch those close around me.

During the day, Dale called me to let me know he would be running a number of errands. He asked me to take my time coming over for the next session, so I decided to pick up a few groceries.

We started our 'work' at about 5:30 p.m.

People have a strong belief that they are each joined together in some way. Some think it is possible that, on a trip to Paris, they will meet someone who is somehow acquainted to a personal friend at home. There is also an underlying belief that no matter where you are going, you will always be recognized.

The universal law of attraction states that, wherever you travel, on a subconscious level, there is a need to attract to people who are your equal. By operating under this law, it is likely you will attract to people who have already travelled to your country, or to people you will meet on your journey. Thus, chances are you will each know the same people. However, you may also travel and not meet someone who shares a same friend or acquaintance, but you still operate under this universal law of attraction.

Often, people believe that travelling is unsafe, or they fear things going wrong when they are travelling. This belief conflicts with the universal law of attraction. Perhaps, the reason for having these fears stems from a past life experience where there were great difficulties when travelling. Like your other limiting beliefs, you must work through these obstacles to overcome your fears.

So, to take another example, you may ask, "If there is a universal law of attraction, why is it difficult to find a relationship? Why is it difficult for someone to attract to me?" But, it is your conflicting beliefs, attitudes and desires that make finding a relationship seem impossible. For instance, a woman may feel ambivalent about getting married because she does not want children. While she would like to get married, she is also aware that her husband-to-be may want children. She knows she will have to care for that child, but this is not what she desires; it is her partner's desire. While society is making small gains, it is still rare for a man to take responsibility for rearing a child. So, instead of attracting the relationship she wants, subconsciously, the woman will justify not having one by assuming she is undesirable. And, in a rather skewed fashion, she achieves her desire of perceived freedom by not having a child in a relationship.

There are other reasons for why the law of attraction does not work. Men, more so than women, have a tendency to look for perfection in a relationship, and are considered more demanding than women. Men expect women to provide, and often, are not willing to compromise. Men are taught to control relationships which results in difficulties establishing one. But, the issue is that men subconsciously desire independence. So, rather than compromise and relinquish control, a man's subconscious beliefs encourage independence. And, in a man's search for perfection, he engages in a number of short-term relationships because they are seemingly perfect at first, then reality and imperfection soon kick in, and the relationship quickly ends.

There are many misconceptions in regards to homosexual relationships. Due to religious beliefs and teachings, many individuals believe that homosexuality is unnatural or sinful. Through conditioning, gay people have subconsciously accepted these wrongful beliefs. In doing so, they believe society does not want them to have relationships, and their relationships will fail because they are perceived to be wrong.

Another conflicting notion about homosexuals, in particular gay male relationships, is that open displays of affection between men are wrong. The result is that heterosexual men often feel threatened, and will react aggressively when they see two men expressing emotions to one other. The belief that any form of affection between males is wrong has been passed down through the centuries. Even in today's society, open affection between two men is seen as unacceptable.

In heterosexual relationships, men trail behind women in personal growth, believing it is unimportant. But, by the year 2000, following a number of environmental catastrophes, men in society will begin to become more aggressive than women in their spiritual development. However, how men and women approach their own personal growth changes is, perhaps, where they will differ the most.

Male energy is a force unto its own; female energy encompasses all. In other words, a woman often protects her man, not vice versa. In relationships, it is a woman who helps the man to understand his relationships with friends, business associates, and even children. It is also usually a woman who explains why the world works the way it does. Yet, men are considered to be the driving force to get their family from point 'A' to point 'B'. Within a relationship, however, men and women work in harmony with each other; they are and must be considered equal.

Over the past 150 years, especially in North America, women have struggled to gain equality. This has led to a breakdown in communication between the sexes, and there has been little compromise or understanding of the changes happening with both sexes. To achieve harmony in relationships, marriages and families, men and women must work together to understand each other and their surroundings. Without communication or a harmonious balance, there can be no satisfying relationships.

Sometimes, however, people use relationships as a way to overlook and ignore their purpose in life. Many believe, subconsciously and to a certain degree consciously, that they would do almost anything for the 'perfect' relationship. However, they often fall short when it comes to taking responsibility for their emotions. To qualify this idea, it is common in relationships for one person to rely on another for happiness and as a cure to their emotional ills. The secret to achieving a solid relationship is to discover first a relationship with yourself. For example, a woman looking for a confident and strong man must learn to develop her male side. She must find the self-confidence and strength within herself before she can attract a partner with those qualities. In turn, a man looking for a sensitive, open and vulnerable woman must learn to develop his female side to the point where he can be sensitive and vulnerable himself. I believe that most people who will be reading this book are women. So, how can a man learn to develop his female side? My response is that all information is universal. You do not have to preach this material to the world because, on a subconscious level, those around you will pick up the message simply by example.

Women must recognize the significance of their purpose in life which is to nurture and help life grow. Women are the benefactors of compassion, sensitivity and vulnerability. Still, so much is being lost, and the difficulties in the world are pushing men and women farther and farther apart. Parents, as well, are having great difficulty with their children as they try to ensure they grow up with the best education and opportunities. But, what consideration is given to a child to enjoy its youth, its creativity, and the need for play both alone or with friends? In your society, children as young as four are strapped into a harness of responsibility; a learning machine is put over their head with expectations of high performance. In reality, it is not the children who are performing, but the parents who manipulate the harness. When children have the opportunity to be creative and are able to learn at their own pace, they will fully appreciate what life has to offer. They will learn compassion and understanding towards others. But, if they are conditioned to be constantly learning or to strive for perfection, they will feel like failures because they can never meet their parents' expectations. Parents do not realize that they are trying to live

26

vicariously through their children and, in turn, parents perpetuate their own parents' expectations and desires. Parents do not understand that there is more at stake than just 'survival of the fittest'. From the parents' perspective, if a child's success is measured solely by his or her abilities, what good is accomplished if the child is unhappy.

We live in society as if in a box. Over the past 100 years, North American cities have been structured in a way that lacks creativity. It is a reflection of what is happening on a metaphysical level. Cities reflect what its inhabitants feel. So why do people feel trapped? I am certain that many want to get out, but to go where? For those who feel trapped, sometimes the only way out is anger, and this can translate into many forms of aggression.

In some countries, there is a belief in controlling people by force. But, if one goes on a strict diet, after four days, the overwhelming urge is to binge. So, if people are restrained by force, after four years, the overwhelming urge is to break the rules.

To create a valuable relationship of any type, you must learn to compromise. Without compromise, there is no relationship. For instance, a relationship created under the expectation that your partner will support you emotionally is unhealthy. People who desire a relationship must first take responsibility for themselves. The age-old belief that women marry men like their fathers, and men marry women like their mothers can lead to very problematic situations. It is unhealthy for men to expect women to look after the children and the home. And, it is also destructive for women to expect men to provide security and consistency. In the end, both parties will be disappointed. Relationships and expectations have not changed from what your parents experienced. If anything, the situation has gotten worse.

Christine, do you want a relationship?

"Yes I want a relationship."

So, what are your motives for wanting a relationship? Is it to make you feel good? Or is it simply a desire for one? People often want a relationship to make them feel good. This is not a 'good' reason on its own.

So, what is the difference in simply wanting a relationship, and wanting one to make you feel good? Wanting a relationship to feel good is a way to feel acceptable in society's eyes.

Simply wanting a relationship is a choice to work on relationship skills. One pursues a relationship to learn responsibility for his or her emotions. Thus, the difference between the two motives is that a real relationship requires work while the 'wanting one to make you feel good' forces someone else to do the work. You can have a solid relationship if you do the work yourself, however, most people will not make the effort because there is too much compromise needed to make a relationship successful.

Consider this: A husband comes home and expects dinner on the table instead of helping his wife with the cooking. If women condone this behaviour because they 'need' to be accepted by society, men will have no reason or motive to change. So, not only are women left with the work, but men are hindered in their growth. Men will be emotionally blocked from taking responsibility for themselves and from recognizing that they need to compromise to share the responsibilities within a relationship.

It takes two to make a relationship work. And, if both partners work outside the home, why should only one be responsible for the chores? Society condones the notion that women are best suited to work inside the home, and men are only the breadwinners. This belief is false. It has been passed down through the centuries. Unfortunately, many overlook these attitudes because to question a patriarchal society is to attack it, and asking such questions is a threat to the status quo. People who criticize society's attitudes are not seen as improving the situation, but rather, looked upon as a menace and punished for their actions. Some of history's greatest people were considered a threat to society. It was only after their death when they were remembered as heroes. But, 'after the fact' is sometimes too late.

Despite the difficulties, society is slowly changing. It is moving towards a new era, a new millennium, where drastic changes will occur quickly. Stand back and reflect within. Ask yourself how you can improve your life for yourself and those around you.

People today have lost their sense of community, and the desire to help each other out. They are living in the 'box'. Yet, it only takes one person to strike the match and burn the box down.

So, Christine, do you still want one?

"I want to learn through a relationship so, yes, I do."

Why don't you make the decision to have one? Twice now you have answered that you want one but will you take the responsibility to create it? So, if I ask the question again, how will you answer me? Will you say, "Yes, I want one," or "Yes, I will create one."

"Yes, I will create one."

Yes, make the choice to create a relationship. I have spoken a great deal about creative expression, and through this discussion of relationships I return again to using creativity to achieve your life's desires. So, with your creative sensibility, you can achieve anything you want. A relationship is a part of creativity for you and the other individual whom you attract. Through the universal law of attraction, you can attract a partner who shares a similar approach to life. Ultimately, what you look for in a relationship is for you to decide.

Subconsciously and consciously, people evaluate what a potential partner in their lives can offer them. Usually, the first question that should be asked about a possible lover is: "Does this person have what I want?" But, the typical questions usually are: "Does this person have beauty? Money? An outgoing personality?" People see relationships in terms of what the other has to offer, and many potential partners are passed over because they appear to offer nothing.

Unfortunately, many consider a person's monetary value instead of the relationship potential. Wealth, physical beauty and a gregarious personality are material achievements. These attributes make you attractive to friends and family. Spiritual development is also material. Therefore, to achieve a relationship without bias, look beyond what you have been taught and allow your 'self' to be drawn to the other person you should really see. A relationship without bias is a catalyst for helping you to achieve your creative inner desires and goals. Through the universal law of attraction, you can draw in a partner who is best suited to you, who will work with you to achieve your purpose. Stop rating people on what they have to offer and make the decision to draw in what it is you actually desire, not what you think you need on a superficial level.

Some may interpret my ideas to mean that they can achieve a relationship by making the choice alone. This is not the complete answer. You must work on your inner 'self' to understand your choices. In the past, it was believed that God or the universal force provided relationships to all those who waited. At one time this was true, but it no longer works today.

A hundred years ago one would enter into a relationship simply to survive. Relationships are no longer needed for that purpose. Therefore, to create what you want, you must incorporate the universal law of attraction, and know you are responsible for your own circumstances. Nothing is destined.

The harder you work on your inner core, the more you can accomplish in life. Don't be alarmed by the word 'work'. This kind of work requires no physical labour, but rather, a mental, emotional and spiritual effort, each a part of creative expression.

By the year 2005, half of North Americans will have fifty percent leisure time to think. To use this time productively, you must come to a point where you can understand how your mind and energy works and how to use them beneficially. Would you consider a paralyzed person in a hospital bed of no use to society? Quite the contrary. Those who are physically immobilized can use their mental power and emotional energy in a different capacity. They are not paralyzed in their evolution or growth. At times, these individuals move mentally much more quickly than their able-bodied counterparts. If you are physically paralyzed, you would be forced to look inward. Yet, you would still desire movement. Therein lies the contradiction—a contradiction of energies. If a person is immobile, he or she does not have a physically mobile energy, but a stronger mental energy. With a stronger mental energy, this person would have the opportunity to evolve mentally at a much quicker rate because they could observe life through eyes much different than someone who is physically able.

Ultimately, a physically immobile person would understand that, while he or she lacked the ability to move, this person could not be trapped; he or she would be safe and protected as an energy force.

Eventually, you will see that you are not trapped in your creative expression. You will realize that you exist on this physical plane, and you are a creative form within yourself.

People fear that their lives are boring and have little to offer. So, allow your life to be mundane and boring, and you still will be happier than the multitudes who are trying to prove their lives are not. People are so rushed to have a number of experiences and possessions that they are missing out on life.

So, now, with all of your material possessions, are you happy? Most might respond, "I am satisfied." But I bet you, few would say, "I am happy." The smart ones, however, would say, "I am content." And, the evasive ones would say, "It just keeps getting better." So, for those who really want to give a meaningful answer would say, "I have to think about it." Those are the ones who get the most out of life, because, at every turn in the road, they are thinking about where they are and where they will go. As a final thought, there is an old expression rarely used anymore, "Think, don't sink."

When we began our session this evening, the doorbell rang within the first ten minutes of dictation, at which point Dale came out of trance. Sarah saw who was at the door but Dale felt the need to see who it was as well. Once he returned, Dale went back into trance, and Seth began again.

I was initially surprised to hear Seth discuss the universal law of attraction. Ironically, earlier in the day, I had thought about the very same subject. Was I being impressed with the forthcoming information of tonight's session?

Seth was so dynamic in his delivery of ideas on relationships that I strongly felt the clarity of his words. I knew that his insight into our underlying and conflicting beliefs was true. During these sessions, I try to apply much of the information to my own life. In particular, memories of the breakdown of my own marriage forced me to think about the many years I spent on my own, enjoying the freedom, the space and the privacy. I wanted another relationship, but I sure was definitely taking my time about it. When Seth spoke about the subconscious beliefs of women, and how they justify not having a relationship because they believe they are unattractive and undesirable, it hit a nerve within me.

There was so much more to look at and to uncover about myself. There is always something challenging to think about in my spiritual development. Slowly but surely, I will continue to unfold that which lies deep within myself.

What was unique in this session was Seth's responses to questions around relationships. I had asked myself many of the same questions when I was in my teenage years and throughout my marriage. For some reason, this sent a chill up my spine.

Dale came out of trance as excited as I was about the material. We talked a little longer about the session.

REPRESSED MEMORIES

*M*onday, May 11, 1998 - I worked leisurely over the weekend spending a great deal of time transcribing Seth's tapes. When I woke up Monday morning I was surprised at how much my lower backside ached.

My original desire during the weekend was to talk to my mother about my birth, my childhood, and the events of my youth. Unfortunately, I did not get around to it; the timing didn't feel right. I now realize I used my 'work' on the book as an excuse not to pursue these issues to delve deeper into my past.

When I arrived at Dale's house after work on Monday, he and Laura were in the kitchen. While Dale was preparing tea for us, he described his weekend and coincidentally mentioned that his lower backside also had been bothering him. I quickly responded that I had the same problem. Dale described his pain as being on the right side and I told him mine was on the left. We both found this strange, and had a good laugh over it.

We worked our way into our chairs as Dale went into a trance and I waited for Seth to come through.

It is I, Seth.

So, you and Dale are perplexed about the pain in your lower backsides.

"Yes."

If I am not mistaken, and this is something you can quote me on if you wish, Jane Roberts and her husband Robert Butts also experienced physical problems when doing certain sessions. It's a connection, on a soul level, for both of you as a result of doing this book. Christine, your pain is on the left side, and Dale's is on the right. It is a balancing act but it will pass. You are dealing with a very sensitive area—unconscious issues—which people do not normally think about. And, your pain is a symptom of the connection between you and Dale. The connection will be even stronger during the course of writing this book.

Today, I wish to talk about repressed memories.

To begin, people believe that repressed memories are either not connected to actual events or are an exaggerated memory of a past experience. But, recognize that people undermine each other's thoughts and beliefs.

If you listen to someone who reveals the memory of a horrendous experience, you may question or even doubt what is being said. One reason for this scepticism is that you have not experienced these situations in your past. People feel a certain distrust for what they have not experienced and repressed memories are similar. People repress childhood memories of events that they, and we, want to believe did not happen because they are too painful to accept. The physical and emotional trauma that transpires from these events often leaves the individual emotionally scarred. Thus, rather than accepting what has happened, the person will distrust and repress the memory of the experience as well as its emotional impact. This memory will remain repressed until the individual feels safe enough to approach the matter and work it out.

For society to reject a person's repressed memories is to again tell this same person that they are not trusted, they do not speak the truth or that their experiences never happened.

So does all of this mistrust come from society, parents or yourself? Look for the reason why you do not trust and you will understand that society doubts the voices of anybody who criticizes its rules and regulations. To go one step further, it is not the person who criticizes, but the actual criticism itself that is seen as a threat. And all criticisms of the status quo are perceived as damaging. However, it is the messenger of this criticism who receives the punishment. Society remains stable by protecting its commonly held beliefs about what is normal and how it should function. To question these norms is to question society's stability. As the new millennium approaches, people are trying to heal themselves and will find a new understanding of what is happening around them. If you are attuned emotionally, mentally, physically and spiritually, you can understand the extent to which society's rules and regulations limit people's progressive nature. The new millennium is about you, the individual; it is about awareness, acceptance, compassion, altruism, philanthropy, and most importantly, self recognition. If you know yourself, you will know others. The principal essence of the Age of Aquarius is best stated as "Know thy self." As I indicated in a previous session, the earliest method of communication was called a 'knowingness'. Once again, this mode of communication will resurface and, in the future, many will utilize this skill.

People with repressed memories may not understand what has transpired in their youth, but they may have a knowingness or a feeling that something terrible happened in their lives. It is only over time, often years, that these memories will resurface again. Whether society or your court system accepts what has happened is not important. In the future, you will understand that the courts do not need to punish those who have harmed you, since people are capable of punishing themselves. And through karmic debt, the perpetrator in this lifetime may go unpunished, but in another place and another time, the perpetrator will bring about his or her own detrimental circumstances and, at the point, must face the actions of this present life.

So, you may ask, "What about those who murder? Should they not be brought to justice?" I am not talking about murder specifically. I am talking more about the perpetrators who abuse children, physically, emotionally, sexually or otherwise. Ironically, child abuse is rarely committed by strangers, however, society still believes strangers commit the abuse, whereas many times it is family, friends or neighbours who are the abusers.

Exploring repressed memories is part of discovering your 'self' in this physical reality. To accomplish this feat requires you to trace your life as far back into your childhood as possible. This pursuit can cause great emotional pain, but the rewards are immense in the long term. The further back you go into your past, the more you will understand yourself and the stronger you will grow since you will understand more strongly your purpose and your limitations. Where there is true acceptance of the 'self', peace and contentment will follow. The pursuit of your youth is more appropriate in later years when the search for self-acceptance and understanding become more important. To wait until later in life, you may find an acceptance within yourself, but there still may not be the contentment you desire.

Society holds a disdain for dealing with issues of one's youth. The reason is simple, society 'looks bad' and must accept the blame if one has been wrongly accused or hurt. But, should not those who have been hurt also have the opportunity to redeem themselves? Is that not a requisite for an open society, to freely voice their pain?

Repressed memories result from not being heard. Children who have been physically and emotionally battered often have no other venue to voice their pain. These individuals recognize the need to voice their childhood ills. If silenced, the pain will continue, and will only perpetuate the silence of others who try to come forward and voice their own pain.

The result is a perpetual pattern of one mistake after another. But, the continuous pattern of wrongdoing does not resolve the problem, only vocalizing the problem will. It is not important whether these repressed memories be accepted by society. What is important is that people who have been abused can accept themselves and be allowed to talk about the horror they have experienced. They must have an opportunity to speak out loud to those who are willing to listen and assist in their healing. If there is no one who will listen, one must find another outlet, such as putting a pen to paper. Despite your doubts or hesitations, as long as you know in your heart that your story is true, you must express your pain.

Adults gladly listen to a child's story if it is entertaining, but they have a difficult time listening to a child describe being beaten and silenced. We only want to hear the entertaining stories but have difficulty listening to the upsetting ones. But, aren't these equally as important?

Listening to Seth this evening, I became more aware of my youth and how I had been silenced. I was troubled by what seemed so emotionally irreparable and the uneasiness that it could not be easily fixed. It was difficult to articulate these feelings. However, as the evening progressed, I clearly remembered the difficulties I had with friends in my youth including an inability to communicate in ways I considered normal. This was the first time during our sessions that I started feeling depressed and hopeless. I felt uncertain as to what these feelings may bring tomorrow.

We continued the session that night into the next chapter.

LIVE AND LET LIVE:
EXPRESSING YOUR CAREER AND YOUR SELF

Monday, May 11, 1998 - (continued)

Standing at the crossroads of change, people search for new careers to gain emotional, mental, spiritual and material satisfaction. Today, many changes are happening in the work place, but people still force themselves into careers they are uncertain of. There is quite a difference between being forced into a career and choosing a vocation that one would enjoy. Imagine a career you chose out of free will that brings contentment and enjoyment. If you try to make something happen you will experience feelings of stress, inadequacy and intellectual doubt.

To prepare for a career can take up to 10 years of post-secondary education. However, it would be dismal to find upon graduation that your selected career is on the downswing or flooded with candidates looking for the same job opportunities. As the year 2000 approaches, people around the world will ask where have all the profitable jobs gone? Many will feel that the real war has begun and will feel the need to fight for survival. Many will be forced into situations where they will find it difficult to survive materially.

North American society has sketched a painting of overall prosperity where its economy is thriving. But it is not because the current economic statistics are painting a false picture. People are living beyond their financial means, with little hope of ever catching up.

There is a definite lack of awareness of the true state of the economy. People have so far focused their attention on their careers and have only started to think about what they are getting from it as far as their skills and talents are concerned.

You must focus upon and discover your abilities to find opportunities you never knew existed. For instance, you may have an affinity for animals and may at some point consider becoming a dog groomer. You may decide to align your business with a veterinarian clinic to create a centre that delivers many different services to similar customers—pet owners. The key to discovery is to follow your desire and the pursuits of your youth can often reveal where your true desires lie.

You may say that you have always wanted to act, but might consider it a foolish dream since there are so many who are actors while you have such little talent. But acting is not the only creative outlet, and may reflect only a part of the whole career. Your desire for an acting career may simply reflect a need to do something creative. You may decide that your talent and desire for performing could be used in the fields of public relations or communications. You may also discover that you have a strong voice, and with training, become a singer. During your pursuit you may find a person who is able to write songs and someone else who has a studio, and, yet, another who can manage and promote your talent. Accordingly, you may find that advertising is a suitable avenue to express your creativity, and you may decide that creating ad campaigns provides an outlet to your creative expression. What I wish to express is that your desires do not have to be limited to just one thing.

Your desire to act may express a desire to be with people, and you may feel that your creative fulfilment can be derived from running a studio that offers acting, dance and art classes. The key element to remember is that if you want to be involved in the arts, do not seek an administrative position where you limit your creative opportunities. A love for the arts does not mean that you must be involved solely in an environment that promotes the arts.

Photography may be regarded as another offshoot of acting which is another form of creativity and a method of earning a living by selling pictures to magazines and other publications.

Finally, writing is another type of creativity, an outlet to express the different characters within yourself and to bring out the actor from within. A street musician is both a musician and actor. It requires an ability to act in front of the many strangers who pass on the street, each with their own judgment of who you are. The expressions on their faces will tell if you are a success or not.

You have been taught to be your harshest critic. And, many believe they are not naturally talented in a particular area, they should not enter that profession. I believe the opposite. If there is something you love and desire, you should work hard to manifest it and create your own unique style.

There is a living soul I see, a Canadian, who goes by the name of Leonard Cohen. At the start of his career he was as a poet, eccentric at best, but not recognizable. Over the years, he put music and voice to his poetry, and again, was at best tolerated as one who is different. Over time, however, society came to understand him and allowed this wonderful poet to persist and be himself, and he has since gained notoriety world-wide, for his music, poetry, creativity and insight.

Are you willing to risk being different, or would you prefer to be like one of many in a herd of cattle that is eventually taken to slaughter? To be different is to stand alone as the only bull in the field, in charge of your own destination. Allow yourself the room to fail in your career. If you assume success is the only goal, failure is not an option. And if failure is not an option, you will not consider any alternate opportunities. From your perspective, any career you choose and enjoy cannot help but fail initially because, as I have already mentioned, in your mind you are your own worst critic. But as you eventually begin to accept yourself, society, in turn, will do the same.

Listen to what others have to tell you. If they tell you that you do not have a good singing voice, use it as fuel to propel you to become a great singer. Leonard Cohen was never noted for his singing, yet many love his unique, vocal abilities.

The same reasoning applies no matter your interests, abilities and talents. There is more than one way to find enjoyable creative expression. Therefore, never become fixed on just one option.

Much like the area of communication, or the language of knowingness, people have lost and repressed their sense of compassion. You must rediscover your creative abilities in order to truly feel again if you show compassion to others. People will learn from your example. However, kindness comes with a high price tag since it is a trait that is often frowned upon. Choose to be kind to yourself when you decide what career it is you desire. Listen to yourself and to others close to you.

Why bother singing if it's numbers you really love? If you are in a career you do not like and there is something you enjoy more, move into that field. If your partner questions why you are changing your career, simply explain that it is something you enjoy.

Women think in terms of love and their emotional needs, while men are viewed as being more tactile. A tactile environment is grounding for men and most find a sense of completeness through physical work. Men forget, however, that women need touch and communication. Therefore, the two sexes ignore one another's needs. Both men and women need to display more compassion, understanding and patience for one another.

If I was married, I would not expect my wife to play football with me. However, if I was smart, I would ask her to watch me play and tell me how I could improve.

If, on the other hand, I was married to a man, I would not want him to attend a baby shower, nor would I expect him to understand what I, and the other women, discussed. But when I arrived home, he might require some love and attention.

Clearly, Seth was poking fun at our sexist society and his humour was coming out by the end of this session. He continued on a personal note.

Years ago, this individual I speak through, Dale Landry, heard that channelling occurred with some people suddenly while they were meditating. Without explanation, a soul would sometimes come through a physical person and start speaking. Dale could not understand why people would believe this because he knew this is not the way it happens. He understood that channelling required practice and a great commitment before a person could channel a soul from spirit, sometimes six months or even six years.

Nevertheless, the myth was created that a spirit could suddenly alight upon a physical person and become a voice of great enlightenment. And many assumed that while meditating they too could channel a soul from spirit who would deliver great words of wisdom.

This example is a reminder of how myths about love are created. Women believe that a man will suddenly appear one day, come out of nowhere and there will be instant love. There are many misconceptions about marriage and relationships. Recognize these false and unworkable beliefs and realize that relationships, love, careers and other achievements all need work to become successful.

Friendships also require work. They require both tolerance and commitment from each person involved as does any relationship. Children also need tolerance, love and commitment. Society as a whole needs love too but suffers from miscommunication between people. Ask yourself what you must do to become successful and bring love, enjoyment and harmony into your life.

Following Seth's dictation, I wanted Seth to answer some of my own questions about love and relationships.

"Where does infatuation fit in? Do we confuse it with love? A relationship appears nice and rosy at first, but then reality sets in."

From what I see, infatuation is an element of boredom.

"Really?"

When you become infatuated with someone, is your life exciting or boring?

"You mean boring before creating infatuation?"

Infatuation. In other words, if your life is something you've created, there is no time for infatuation.

"Hmm."

Do you understand my philosophy? It may be difficult to believe that infatuation grows out of boredom, but if you exercise more caution with your feelings, there would be fewer assumptions made about love.

When you are infatuated, chances are you are not being realistic about what the other person can offer you. Infatuation implies that you see the other person as a perfect partner, a "dream boat," but the dream boat sinks fast when reality sets in.

Until I shall have another opportunity to speak with you again, may god speed you towards enlightenment.

"Thank you."

SILENCING

*T*uesday, May 12, 1998 - I was having an exceptionally good day.
Nothing in particular happened to make me feel so elated, however
I was enjoying it tremendously.

*I had thought about how I could approach my mother with the
intimate questions about my childhood. I wasn't sure whether she would
want to discuss the subject. I felt that, she may, after all, prefer to leave
the matter in the past or may not even remember the events clearly.*

*Just prior to leaving work for Dale's place, one of my co-workers
started up a conversation. Even though I wanted to get going, I had the
impression that being slightly late would not be a problem, so we
continued talking. My intuition was right. Dale was on a business call
when I arrived and our session started late. I had time to make tea; no
one else was at his home.*

*Once Dale finished and we finally settled into our chairs, he
surprised me with his remark. He too was feeling elated.*

*As Seth began speaking through Dale, I had the distinct impression
that something very out of the ordinary was going to transpire.*

Looking at their past, some people do not see how they have been
silenced from voicing their thoughts. They don't see that living in a

capitalist society demands a robotic approach to life, to desires and to needs. Upon a closer look, can it not be said that society has taught everyone to desire material goods?

Would you consider a relationship with someone who you did not see as beautiful or successful? Almost daily your artistic and expressive natures are stifled or silenced. In your society, you no longer teach yourself to be who you are, but rather to be who you think you need to be in order to succeed. If you live a mechanical life with little meaning or depth, you will find a relationship that lacks individuality.

Now you may say, "I am always attracted to people who are different. I look for individuals who are thinkers. I make my own choices." In response, I say, argue for your limitations, especially if you feel the need to defend yourself against the ideas I present to you.

Regardless of what you believe while reading this book, simply ask yourself these questions: Am I getting what I want out of life? Am I creating what I really want? Have I been silenced?

If you have been silenced, you need to reawaken your thought process and see life through different eyes. You must develop a greater clarity within yourself about what you want to achieve.

It is said that you do not understand denial until you come out of it. It is the same for one who has been silenced. You will not be aware of the extent of your silence until you find your voice. What is most important in life is to find a sense of fulfilment and contentment with knowing who you are and what it is that you want. If you desire what others also want, so be it; there is no harm in that. However, if you are constantly dissatisfied, you are not looking for fulfillment in the right spot. If you find life is empty or feel unconnected to the people around you, you have somehow gone astray but can still learn from these mistakes.

If you realize that your marriage is not what you want, the solution may not necessarily be to leave your partner to find yourself. Rather, you have to take responsibility for your own decisions. Discuss with your partner what it is you both want, as individuals, and find a solution you can both live with. Ensuring your children's well being is also essential, for they are a part of you, a part of what you've created. To deny them the love and protection they need is to also deny these things to yourself.

Family life is not solely about women taking care of children. Too often, women assume the role of child rearing because they believe no one else will take responsibility, and this may very well be the case, but more importantly, it is about two adults, not one, sharing the responsibility. Together, problems can be solved, but if there is no communication there is no solution.

Usually, men are taught to speak when angry, and often times say little. This is one aspect of men being silenced. Women are taught to speak whenever they want, but often say nothing which is another form of silencing. So, who is being heard and where did these beliefs about silencing originate? Have you asked yourself where your thoughts and feelings even come from? Does God put thoughts into your mind? Is there something beyond your mind? How does your mind and thought process work? Are you planted in bodies and then there is nothing else? Does God flip a switch and you, like a robot, begin to operate?

There is more to life than just your career, but to know what it is, you must search and find its meaning. If you do not seek, you will not find. Answers come only when there is thought behind the question and a desire for the answer.

At one time, only those of means and power could read, write and communicate intellectually, or so it was believed. Thus, the lower classes were presumed ignorant. But over time, people have broken free of these limitations and beliefs, have become educated and can now think for themselves and learn to have desires. But, if people are truly free, why do so few think for themselves? Why do so few know what it is that they truly desire?

Accomplish your soul's desire and you will feel complete. But first you must discover what it is your soul desires. Is it a marriage and children? Do you want to be an actor? A writer? A chemist? Is it to know yourself? Why are you here? Are you wandering through life not knowing where you are going or what you are looking for? A recipe for discontentment, I am sure. Can you imagine how different the world would be if everyone understood their purpose and desires? Perhaps to some, living is a purpose for understanding while others have closed off their minds to their desires.

There are people who desire to travel and that alone has its purpose. Uncover your capabilities, learn more about your 'self', your desires, your thought processes and how to work with them, and you will have a far richer life. The first desire for many Americans under age fifty is wealth and financial independence. Secondly, there is a desire for security and a successful career. And, thirdly, there is a desire to know more about one's self, one's family and one's friends.

I believe that people have their priorities backwards. Topping the list should be family, community and knowing the self. The second priority is career and no matter how many different careers you have, keeping it your second priority will keep you in good standing throughout your life. From these two priorities comes the third which is financial success. Many people will laugh at this re-order of priorities but, at age 65, you will see the value of this arrangement. At 65, you have time to focus within and think back about what has transpired in your life. You will likely believe that too much time has been wasted trying to find success instead of finding your inner self. This is another part of the silencing imposed on people throughout their lives. One is being silenced by having a skewed perspective on these priorities without knowing it. For others, the desire for spiritual knowledge parallels a desire for wealth, fame and recognition, which is the desire is to stand apart and remain untouched.

Each person is unique and individual. At one time, only the 'elite' had status because they had both power and means. They stood alongside royalty. Today, people see that even royalty is fragile, but at one time, money and status could hide those flaws and today money no longer hides anything. The public seeks out the rich and famous with a vengeance, wanting to know everything in their private lives. In many ways, those who truly stand apart are tortured because they have no privacy or individuality; a sad situation, yet a situation many crave.

If I existed on your physical plane, my goal would be to own a small cottage with a flower garden and a close friend next door. Everyday I would have someone to talk to, share tea and enjoy the beauty of nature. I would landscape my garden, with all of its flowers and plants to show off their beauty and radiant colours. For work, I would sketch portraits of my garden and sell them to city strangers who desired a small piece of my world. And with each portrait, I would include the essence of my good fortune and life's many splendours, including my goals and my purpose.

You do not need to read books to gain wisdom, or to read newspapers to know what is happening in the world. You need to think and to have a voice. If your picture of contentment is significantly different from what I have previously described, do you truly understand your purpose?

What followed was another discussion between Seth and myself.

Does it sound like I am preaching?

"It's a little slow." For much of the session up to this point, I had felt quite drowsy and unable to keep my eyes open.

It appears slow because to really get the most out of life, one has to slow down.

"I should have seen this coming."

Yes, I think you just got hit by a truck and that is the whole point. Most don't see it coming and don't understand that they need to slow down if they are going to accomplish the things in life that are more enriching. Some days are full, others half full, and sometimes the half full days are as important as the full ones, because if you don't recognize that you have half full days, you'll never the see the fullness in a full day.

"I understand that, I think!"

Before I finish this book, you must remind me that I want to allow Jane Roberts to come through Dale, because she does have her own views. I hope that people will not find it blasphemous that I ask her to assist me in this way. The reason I want her to speak is because she is viewed by many as an individual who has made incredible strides in the field of channelling. To not allow her through would be like assuming that Christ did not exist.

Jane Roberts and Robert Butts gave freely of themselves so others could find their song and learn to sing. They unlocked the unconscious and subconscious minds for many people. Even though their initial desire to know more about themselves may have appeared selfish, they opened a kaleidoscope of knowledge, thoughts and beauty that even they never expected was there. In so doing, they unleashed their own power and gave others the opportunity to do the same. It is not my objective to glorify or praise them. Rather, I wish to show them as two souls who took a risk and should be recognized and respected for this distinction, just as you need to recognize and appreciate the similar qualities in yourself.

A man may work on a farm his entire life and be truly satisfied until someone criticizes and tells him it is not enough. People are often told that the way they live their lives is unsuitable. But these people must ask themselves whether it is suitable to them, and discover for themselves what they want to master in life.

It is better to be with someone who wants to be himself or herself rather than with someone who only wants wealth and success. Wealth and success lead to a life of torment. Be yourself and you will constantly change your colours. Enjoy the changes and live each moment to the fullest.

When you can capture the moment, you need not look further because the moment offers everything. The moment offers a mirror of who you are and a sense of contentment. But even after that first moment, there is another, and then another. One moment is one thought, and each flows into the next creating an array of different thoughts, all linked together to express new ideas, new pathways, new changes. I would be damned to sit still in my thoughts if I lived in a physical reality such as yours. Can you not see your blindness? Can you not understand you are living in a barren wasteland created by you? Your neighbour did not create it. Your government did not create it. You have created it. It is up to you to change what is in your life if you do not enjoy it. Adopt an alternate lifestyle, create a different reality, create anything that will bring you fulfilment and contentment. Express a different side to yourself, a side that will show you what you are here to accomplish.

I have had the opportunity to live in your physical reality but I chose not to because I'm not sure I could stand the constant enjoyment of living life in the moment.

Seth looked at me and smiled. His sense of humour is often revealed during sessions.

You do not see the possibility for choice. You say, "If I had." But you

50

do have. Whether it is in your mind or in your body, the reality is there to create. You limit that reality and yourself.

If I am not mistaken I believe the glass has just become full.

"It did."

Jane Roberts is here. With this soul's, Dale Landry's permission, I will let her through to speak, and I am glad that you reminded me.

"I thought Jane would come through Dale at some future time."

Is this not some time in future? The future has just met the present.

"That's twice in one night."

I enjoy your mental frailty, it is refreshing.

"Hmm."

Jane came through. There was a definite change in Dale's appearance as Jane's personality emerged. As I could see and sense in Dale's expression, the entity of Jane seemed poised and excited as she readied herself to speak. She spoke slowly.

This environment is not new to me, but the circumstances for which I am being called upon are far different than from my own past experience. Seth offers me many avenues of choice but I prefer to follow him to see which route he takes and to see if it will also expand my horizons. I believe that if it is good for him, it will only be better for me.

I have no expectations for being here. Some may ask, "How do I know this is Jane Roberts?" In response, I say they will not. Those who knew me from the physical reality may have more reason to ask since they have an emotional attachment which goes far beyond the physical. They may even demand to know why I am here. But instead ask yourself why these circumstances have come about. Ask yourself what inner confusion, what turmoil or upset arises? Then, ask yourself how does it assist me in my growth? How does it help me to get to where I need to be in my life?

It is unimportant in what reality I exist. It is unimportant what pathway I have taken after death. It is also unimportant whether you assume I am joined with Seth, God, or everyone else as one. If I could see myself from your physical reality, I would say "What a unique voice I have in spirit." What a different personality. What a different possibility." And, I would conclude that the soul, Dale Landry, who has allowed me to come through him is in some way similar, just as I was when I existed in your physical reality. He likes a challenge. He likes a different perspective. He likes to know what is happening beyond his doorway. At night when he goes to bed, he either leaves the door open or closed. The choice is his just as the choice was mine, and still is.

I have never been one to mince words, and that part of me will never change, even if every other molecule has. There is a part of each soul which remains the same despite the different physical, mental, emotional and spiritual changes. Travelling through a galaxy of dimensions, too many to express in words, I have discovered something new about Seth. Do you wish to know what it is?

"Yes I do."

I realized that when Seth spoke, he had one train of thought, and when I came through Dale, I also had one train of thought. Yet, Seth's thought and my thought were similar but different. He is similar but different to each of us. Some time ago, I realized that Seth, though a different personality, is, was and will always be a reflection of myself, a multitude of different personalities that I could be and am. Each person is a multitude of the different personalities that can be expressed if he or she desires it. I want to say, know the multitude of personalities that reside within your self, within your conscious and subconscious minds, within your different realities, and understand that they can each be expressed.

To take it one step further, love has so many different expressions, and death is just one part of it.

Jane ended here and Seth once again came through Dale to complete the chapter.

I now understand why I worked so often with that woman. But for now, I close. Until once again we shall have a voice together, may you light upon your purpose and understand your soul.

"Thank you."

My underlying feeling that something unusual would happen proved to be correct and a part of me wished that I could have such clear intuition all of the time.

Jane Roberts speaking through Dale was a true delight, and speaking honestly, there were times I felt like crying due to the emotion I felt when she spoke.

It was obvious to me that there was an undeniable bond between Seth and Jane as one spoke after the other. It wasn't clear to me at first, but as the session ended, what each of them had said to me impacted me deeply. I felt very much as if they were giving me a message that soon I would find my own voice and freedom. But still, I felt bound and tied to my restrictive life, and the way I was living it.

It seems funny as I am speaking about it now, but after listening to Jane, a part of me felt like I also wanted to be in spirit, free from the pain and restrictions I had grown up with.

Even though Jane's life seemed much more difficult than mine, there was an undeniable connection that came through her which left me with a sense of satisfaction when we closed the session.

TWIN SOULS

Wednesday, May 13, 1998 - Laura was planting flowers in the backyard when I arrived, and Dale and Corinne had gone across the road for coffee. I felt a little uneasy this evening and anxious to start our session. Dale arrived soon after and the four of us stayed outside for awhile. Dale discussed how angry he had been feeling all day. I hadn't felt particularly angry but I was uncomfortable. Perhaps, I was denying an underlying anger or upset feelings.

We were ready to start recording by 5:30 p.m.

I have some news. I believe that this Friday both of you will probably have a bit of a bang and I'm not talking sexually either.

Both of you will have similar experiences or parallel events, revelations and insights as you work together on this book.

The next two days will probably bring about some clarity in ways neither of you will expect.

One reason for channelling this book is to cause some irritation. For many people, a feeling of irritation will make them think and this can lead to change. This is not to say that you should irritate people to make them think. Irritating others will make them angry, and they in turn may get angry back at you. However, an irritation can result as one's thoughts are provoked. For instance, you may not feel completely comfortable after reading the information in this book but may not understand why. Keep this in mind when reading.

However, you might enjoy reading this book but then find yourself angry after finishing it. You may have no idea why you are furious since anger can arise from the changes occurring on a subconscious level. This book can give you the "push" you need to change and may provide you the insight that you have been looking for. In essence, you have drawn in the experience. Since you chose to pick up this book and read it, on some level you must desire change. But now, you must deal with the changes that are happening on a subconscious level. You must begin to face your fears, your past and your problems. This realization may bring up a lot of anger, and anger often protects you from seeing the truth, painful memories and feelings. Anger may arise before realizing that you are upset over something that you may have read or due to a past memory.

Seth's delivery was very fast.

Anger is repetitious and can keep you guessing. If you feel angry at a friend or a loved one for no particular reason, you may, upon reflection, realize that that person said something to make you upset. However, you are not really angry at the person, but rather at what they said which triggered something within you, such as your vulnerability. Anger directed towards another person is really a feeling of being out of control, a feeling of being unprotected and a fear of getting hurt. People use anger for protection. To resolve your anger you must be aware of how you use it unnecessarily to protect yourself against what you perceive as harmful. For instance, you may become angry because you believe a friend is manipulating you. But if you think about it, your friend's personality may remind you of someone from your past such as your father who may have hurt you. This memory of your father may trigger a subconscious feeling when you were manipulated or lied to. Therefore, your reaction may be to strike out at your friend, not because he is manipulating you, but because he triggered your anger towards your father. Thus, in the heat of the moment, you may feel justified in projecting your anger towards your friend, but later you may feel remorse and guilt when you realize this person did not try to hurt you. Unfortunately, it may be too late to repair the damage your anger has caused.

There are few individuals who have come from a relatively normal background where both parents were mentally, physically, emotionally and spiritually healthy. Furthermore, few people are raised by parents who were truly responsible, who respected each other's independence, and who did not abuse tobacco, alcohol or their children.

I am equating normalcy with the model society has created, not with what I see as normal. Normal to me is dealing with the situation as it is. If your child has a learning disability then you must approach him or her much differently then you would for one who is 'normal'.

People are raised in families with a deficiency of love, respect, sincerity and boundaries. Many grow up with little physical, spiritual, mental and emotional health. And few experience emotional security, where they are respected for expressing their ideas and where they can discuss their feelings and thoughts without being scolded or criticized as ignorant or weak.

When you recognize your childhood limitations, the immediate response is a desire to replace or recreate what was lost. You may feel angry about the time lost or the lack of contentment. But, it is important to recognize that you can follow your own road to contentment with a sense of yourself and find an understanding of your anger and upheaval. Through this effort, you will see that others are dealing with the same problems. Society teaches you to welcome the many people who come into your life, but not to explore beyond their emotions. You are not allowed to be creative, to delve into personal issues and to see behind the mask. Therefore, you are blind to what actually exists beyond the surface.

You have been taught that if you delve too deeply and ask too many personal questions, others will become angry with you. I am here to say that it is not an abuse to use your intuitive senses to uncover the emotional and personal side of another individual. This is not crossing personal boundaries. You can look beyond the surface and you have a right to look beyond the surface of those who are a part of your life. You have a right to investigate, just as they do.

You will discover many things by looking closely at yourself. The more you see beyond the mask of others, the more you will see a reflection of yourself, and the more you will learn about what goals you want to accomplish.

'Discovery' is not about finding a sunken treasure. 'Discovery' is about finding pieces of yourself as you move along your path.

At this point, Seth gave me the title for this chapter: Twin Souls.

Twins have a unique relationship. They have a special understanding of each other, an intuitive and instinctual link beyond words. They know each other so completely that few discussions are needed.

There is a 'knowingness' between twins much like the lost language I spoke of in a previous session. This knowingness comes from having spent a number of lifetimes together, whether they lived as husband and wife or as lovers. As twins in this lifetime, they instinctually know each other. They come in as twins to be joined together because there is an unspoken love and knowingness. There is a link beyond the love, and this link carries them throughout this life where they will rarely stray far from one another. If they do, they will be quickly reunited; most of the time, this is what transpires. If one twin dies, the other feels incomplete and will sense that he or she has lost a part of themselves. This loss goes beyond the emptiness and pain of losing a loved one. Twins are the only souls who can use the language of knowingness in its complete form, for they encompass what you would understand as a 'oneness'.

People often seek the emotional experience of twins in their love affairs. They want the same relationship that twins have in their knowingness of one another. But, rarely will you find the sense of completeness in a love relationship that twins have. When twins come into their physical bodies, they come as one soul that splits upon entering this physical reality. You and your lover are two separate souls, and there is never the same level of harmony between two separate souls as there is between one soul that has split.

Twins do not use each other for romantic love since that is not their purpose. On one level, their purpose is fulfilled by living as twins in this physical reality. Despite the knowingness between them, they still will not seek to know better each other's desires and accomplishments. They will also experience a sense of completion through their other half, their twin.

As adults, twins may move far away from each other, marry and choose separate careers, but by age seventy, after living a full life, they may come together again in order to feel complete once more. With twins, there is a completeness that others cannot relate to. It is difficult to obtain this sense of completeness. The completeness experienced by twins can be sensed by others close to them. Twins' family and friends may feel this sense of completeness, and incorporate it into their own lives.

Twins can have different personalities despite sharing the same soul, the same mother and the same birth date. When the soul splits, the personality splits and travels in different directions, much like how your soul splits from lifetime to lifetime. Setting aside my discussion about twins, each soul separates from lifetime to lifetime in order to learn something different, such as a new purpose. Eventually, the souls which have split from each other will come together as one to utilize all the information it has learned from all of the lives.

There is a completeness that goes beyond this physical reality that you also strive for to allow you to feel you have achieved your purpose here. You look for a relationship to give you that sense of completeness, but you must discover this sense for yourself; no one can give it to you.

There is a belief that when you reach heaven you will find that sense of completeness. Reaching heaven, however, has nothing to do with feeling complete. When you begin to understand that the world as a whole and all things living on this physical plane are 'one', then you will achieve that sense of completeness. All living things are a part of you, whether you perceive this in your conscious mind or not.

Find a partner who, rather than 'making you happy', will give you comfort. I do not mean material comfort, but the comfort of complementing who you are. A shy, introverted person may find comfort in an outgoing and extroverted partner who can draw him out. But the extroverted partner may find comfort in a shy companion who brings an element of calm to their life. In this way, the two partners complement each other and will obtain balance and harmony.

Finding a similar partner can be very enjoyable initially. But in the long run, it may prove difficult because when two people have much in common they can become lost in their own world with no one to pull them out.

People often ask questions like, "What's wrong with me? Why do I have a problem attracting a partner?" Some even criticize their partner, believing the other is too controlling, unwilling to commit, too manipulative or doting. Each situation has its own extenuating circumstances. However, what is lacking is clear communication between both parties.

I have outlined the following simple rules that, if followed, will help you achieve a more meaningful relationship.

Firstly, if you give someone your phone number and he or she doesn't call within two or three days, this person is not interested in a relationship with you. But if the person calls after two or three days, he or she may be someone who enjoys manipulating others and keeping their emotions hidden. You will never get a commitment or an honest emotional response from this type of person.

Secondly, you must ask yourself if this person you've started dating is kind and considerate. If he or she is not, you have likely drawn in someone who mirrors the pain of your childhood. People in relationships often reflect each other's childhood issues. Therefore, it is up to you to decide if you want to endure the pain of your childhood again or work through these issues.

Thirdly, you don't need to have sex the first time you meet someone. It is an option, but if you want something more, don't have sex at the start. Keep it simple, and don't feel that you have to explain yourself. Your dating partner will eventually figure you out.

Fourthly, avoid a negative attitude as no one likes a 'whiner'. If you blame the world for your relationship problems, be assured that there are plenty of people who will point it back at you. Keep a healthy perspective about everyone you meet.

Fifthly, give people at least three chances, even if you feel that they are unattractive. It can take as many as three dates to discover who a person really is. People usually hide their emotions early in a relationship because they fear being hurt and you may find the person you date more attractive if you just give him or her a chance.

In regards to sex, your society's beliefs around love-making are antiquated. Religion has taught you to feel guilty about sex because it is seen as a sin.

Men see casual sex as a conquest and struggle with the idea of how to make a relationship last and allow themselves to love another person. For women, casual sex brings about feelings of inadequacy.

Sex is present in your everyday life, in advertising, entertainment and the media. Animals are not burdened with society's beliefs about right and wrong and therefore have sex because it is natural. It is not that people believe that sex is unnatural, but they are restrained by the mixed messages surrounding it. To find an answer to problems one is having with relationships requires looking at how you interpret society's ideas around sex.

Some believe it is quite blasphemous to say that the church, religion or society is repressed by its own rules, regulations and standards. You, alone, must take responsibility for your choices, judge what you believe and choose how you want to live your life. You can live life to the fullest by reflecting on and overcoming the guilt that holds you back.

Shortly in the future, all people will be living under one roof, with one government and will be forced to see things in one way. In that moment, you will understand what I say.

At that point in the session, Seth began speaking to me directly.

This is not what you were expecting today but people can never learn enough about relationships. There is always more they want to know. The more people know about personal relationships, the more they feel uplifted and confident that they can find a way out of the chaos society has created. Do you follow me?

"Yes."

As we continue with these session, more of your issues will begin to surface, and the reasons why you hide from the world will become clearer. You will begin to understand your feelings of inadequacy. You now feel it is easier to be alone than to face your ignorance, your pain and your guilt.

"I know that."

Are you willing to change?

"I am."

In one year we will see what has changed. I am not condemning or condoning you. I am simply showing you the test results. What you do is up to you. I will tell you more about your problem and where it originated. This will be an important revelation because if you know where the problem originates, you can start to solve it.

Sometimes you feel shame because you think you are inferior to others even though you are not. In fact, it is not that you are inferior, rather it is your sense of shame that causes you to feel this way. Do you see what I am saying?

"I think so."

If you feel shame around sex, does that make sex wrong or is it that you have just been taught to feel shameful?

"Taught to feel shameful."

Right. Yet, you still believe that sex is wrong.

"Yes."

You believe you are doing something wrong when in fact it is the belief you have been taught that is wrong. You may believe you are less intelligent because you have been told that but you are not in reality. Therefore, it is your beliefs that are limiting. Do you understand?

"Yes."

Something tells me you do understand this time. I am going to close.

The tape ran out before Seth could finish.

I could not deny that Seth had reached a sensitive area within myself, one that I have not been able to resolve for years. In each of my personal relationships, I wanted to project the idea that I had a healthy attitude towards sex, but invariably what surfaced was my shame and guilt.

After the session, I took a long route driving home. I could still feel the pain (or was it fear) and wanted to cry. I thought mostly about the loss I was feeling. I had been living alone and hiding for the past eight years. Home had become my sanctuary, a place to be myself. Was this really how I wanted my life to continue? Had I just been feeling sorry for myself all these years with no intention of changing the outcome? Did I honestly believe that I was content with the way my life was?

There was always an underlying feeling that I was missing out on a more fulfilling and rewarding life somehow.

I am still amazed at how these sessions stir my emotions and bring forth so many thoughts and fears. What a healthy exercise it is to discover one's self.

Thursday, May 14, 1998 - No session was held today. However, I was still processing a great deal of material from the previous night's session.

At around ten this morning, I started feeling tired and frustrated. I found myself thinking about my mother. She is usually the first person I relate to at times of despair.

My mother moved in with me more than two years ago, and our first year together was extremely difficult for me. Even though I had been working on my inner 'self' over the past fifteen years, I was still unprepared for what awaited me when she came into my home.

Observing and understanding life from a distance brings a certain amount of insight, but the actual experience of living together with her brought up emotions and a deeper recognition of my life. I hadn't realized the extent of our similarities. I was in fact a carbon copy of my mother. For years, I truly believed I was different, with different ideas and beliefs. I was wrong. Through our conversations, I was constantly alerted to the extent of how so many of her beliefs and issues were adopted by me.

I was constantly shocked by the revelations of our similarities. My expectations, methods of manipulation, desire for control, emotional neediness and many more other issues were very similar to hers. Accepting my issues was often a struggle and there were many occasions when I wanted my life to return to the way it was before my mother moved in when I had my own space and privacy in tact.

I realize that having my mother live with me provided me the opportunity to resolve matters of the heart, mind and soul. It was obvious that my mother was actually a gift, and not an enemy like I had initially thought.

ALTERING PHYSICAL REALITIES

Friday, May 15, 1998 - I had a chiropractor appointment this evening and didn't show up at Dale's place until sometime after six o'clock. I walked into the kitchen when I arrived to find Sarah, Corinne and Dale sitting around the table discussing the arrangements for our upcoming trip to Maine. Rick showed up shortly thereafter and Dale prepared tea for the both of us and we were ready for our session to begin. As usual, we wondered what material Seth would cover.

Interestingly, the tape recorder was acting up and there was a high pitched sound coming from it. Dale came out of trance to adjust it. Once it was fixed, we resumed our session without further interruptions.

In the future, you will know and understand the many physical dimensions that are unknown right now. These physical dimensions are unpredictable and the knowledge of them will be available in many different forms. For example, within twenty to thirty years, technological and medical advancements will allow people to greatly improve their physical well-being.

While the ability to increase one's physical strength is possible today, it is a lengthy process, sometimes taking one or two years to achieve and requiring the help of a skilled and knowledgeable physician. But in future, simple tests, such as blood and hair tests, will allow people to quickly gain body strength. In this way you will be able to rapidly alter your physical reality. The ability to alter your body strength is available now, but information on how to do this has not been fully accessed and is currently not available to most.

Within the same time frame, some people will develop the ability to send their thoughts telepathically to others, much in the same way computers communicate with other computers. Within fifty to 100 years, people will actually be equipped and trained to send telepathic messages. At this point, you will not understand how it will be used, or even why.

Telepathic abilities are not new. People can project their thoughts to another person. For example, feelings of attraction can be communicated telepathically. So, if someone is attracted to you, he or she will send out a type of 'energy thought' that communicates an interest in you. You then receive this energy and sense the other person's attraction. People underestimate their ability to send or receive telepathic messages. They may pretend that someone else cannot pick up the information, but I am sure you can sense a message coming from someone who is attracted to you, regardless of whether the other person believes in telepathic abilities.

In future, society will use telepathy to send thoughts because it will be both accessible and less costly. More importantly, telepathic powers will become part of society's focus on discovering the full potential of the human brain, a focus that will last for the next 1,000 to 2,000 years.

People will want to take advantage of the many discoveries made in the new millennium. These discoveries—these new assets—are still unknown to the corporate world and, therefore, have not yet been patented. In some cases they never will be. In twenty to thirty years, companies will attempt to patent certain human abilities, but they will be unsuccessful because these abilities are too nebulous and inaccessible in the physical form, and the legal system can only control or rule on physical facts. These problems will continue until society learns to accept the 'human' form of knowledge and learning, and to access the mind.

Another physical reality not yet available is the ability to utilize one's vocal pitch. At one time, when man and woman first inhabited the

66

earth, the voice was used to communicate pictures, and like singing, people adjusted the pitch and tone of their voice accordingly. Within the next thirty to seventy years, the human voice range will increase from eight to fifteen octaves. As these changes occur into the new millennium, the range and vibration of the human voice will also follow suit, and new higher pitches will be found. It is difficult to describe the change in sound or the effect it will have, but these changes will occur.

Human sight will also change and evolve. As people develop their spiritual and psychic abilities, their visual abilities will adjust, and they will develop the ability to literally see into the metaphysical realm. People will classify it as another dimension, or another reality.

At one time, people were able to physically dematerialize their body and move into spirit. When a person died and the body was no longer of use in this physical reality, the body would decompose or dematerialize before the soul moved into spirit. But, when a soul came from spirit to live in this physical reality, it would attempt to stay as long as possible. However, when the body broke down or was no longer working, the person would draw together the elders for a ceremony—a funeral of sorts—to celebrate the time the soul existed in this physical world. In this way, death was celebrated as a joyous occasion. Following the celebration, the body was transcended into spirit. In truth, only the soul transcended into spirit and the body would decompose. The soul felt safe through this experience because as it altered its energy to move back into the spirit world, the physical body itself was also altered.

People fear death today because the body is left in this physical reality while the soul moves into spirit. With this transformation known as death, there is a disconnection from spirit that frightens people because they are forced to leave the physical body behind. In time, as you learn to change the physical energy of your body, you will be able to also move your body into spirit if you so desire. However, as you learn and understand more about the spirit world and as you achieve the ability to visualize both the physical and spiritual realities, you will understand where you are going and will not feel the need to take your body with you. In future, many gifts will be available, but each person must decide which abilities and gifts he or she wants.

It will take people from ten to twenty years to learn how to change their energy from the physical to the spirit realm and vice versa. Less time will be needed for future generations to learn this ability. In thirty to forty years, the children of parents who know how to change their energy, will learn the ability quickly. If parents use their ability to dematerialize, their children, by about age twenty, will take only five years to learn it.

Everyone is psychic but few have learned to use their gifts. For those who have learned to use their gift, they can teach others to do the same. In the end, all people will understand that psychic abilities are simply an altering of their physical energy. By using your psychic ability, your energy will change and rise to connect with spirit. For example, imagine using a ladder to climb to the roof of a very tall building. As you climb the ladder, rung by rung, your view of the world below changes, yet the world itself remains unchanged. By the time you get to the roof, your breathing may have changed, you may be tired from the climb, and there may be other changes you are unaware of. In a similar way, your view will be altered as you change your physical energy to connect with the energy in the spirit world. As your energy changes, your view of the world also will change. Yet in your own thoughts, you are not changing physically. Your energy changes as you move higher into the metaphysical realm; there is less need for air as your body adapts and slows down. As the body's energy increases, it will not become more excited, but will transform itself figuratively into a 'cocoon'.

I don't believe I must defend what I say. In the last twenty years, even the greatest sceptic has changed his opinion on a number of topics. However, what is changing the most are people's views of God, spirit, the universe and what is beyond.

Today, people have a deep need or craving for spiritual knowledge. It is as if they have been living in the dark for years and suddenly sense that there is light up ahead. They know it exists and are looking for it, and will know when they see it. The key to obtaining spiritual knowledge is to know what is right for you as an individual. Some seek knowledge from teachers, others search for it in books, and others will achieve it through friends. Know that if you are looking, you will find it, but you won't if you don't look. With the coming changes to this planet's physical energy, many people will be forced to look beyond—whether they want to or not. Your perception, reality and physical energy will change and you will begin to see things differently.

A final change will be the body's ability to heal itself. Those who become health practitioners will also learn the ability to self-heal. However, it will be a difficult and lengthy process that will require great commitment, making it one of the more 'expensive' changes. The reason for this 'expense' is that the body's energy must dramatically change to heal itself.

To heal yourself, you must experience an inner death, a sense that you are dying. Those who are close to you may sense subconsciously that they are losing you, and your physical energy will also alter and change. This process will be emotionally and physically painful, but through it you will learn compassion, empathy and how to help others.

As with many of these changes, you will learn to balance your energy so that you can relate to another person without feeling the need to control him or her. You will learn to set aside your differences and struggles to find a sense of inner power. The secret to success is not in your power, but in your individuality.

Christ often said to those who came to be healed, "Heal thy self." He was speaking of people's inner power to heal themselves. Allow yourself to discover and use that knowledge, and to look inwardly.

I believe that Christ existed, not as a leader, not as the son of God, but as someone who knew his purpose, his direction, his heart, and cared about the concerns and welfare of those around him. Christ emulated what all people strive for. In the future, you will also achieve these goals. There is nothing Christ did that you cannot do. He did not exist to free you from your sins. He existed to show you how to rid yourself of the darkness and despair of this physical world. He was a messenger, but messages come at a high price because, to this day, many people look to him for answers rather than looking to themselves.

This is not blasphemy, it is merely information. I am not trying to prove what is right or wrong. I am simply giving information. Throughout the centuries, the belief in God has created great pain and destruction. If people could put aside their religious beliefs and love unconditionally those around them, there would be no need to fight over God. Beliefs cause pain, not one's love of God. Recognize the difference between a belief in God and what God truly means to you. If God has given birth to each of you, then each of you descend from God's blood. You are all members of one family, some older, some younger, but all conceived in love.

Many people pray to a God, whatever their concept of God is, and their God is always above them. What many do not see is that God is an energy just like you have an energy, and your prayers are a desire to return to the energy known as God; its oneness and completeness. Again, I am not asking you to accept this information as truth. Let your heart and soul question the information and leave your mind to absorb it.

How did you find the information?

"Very good."

I'm not sure whether you just get high from it or from the energy, or both.

"Both"

But you certainly do seem to hop on that 'energy' sleigh and ride with it.

"Uh huh."

It does seem to have its flavour. How are you finding it as you transcribe these sessions?

"It has been emotional."

Emotionally healing or emotionally insightful?

"Both. I find that when I transcribe the sessions the information takes on a different meaning than when I first heard it."

Let's suppose in ten years down the road this book becomes a huge success and you're in the background saying to everyone, "Hey, I sat in on that. I was there." But, instead no one listens or no one notices.

"That will be fine."

So what are you doing right now, in this moment?

"Participating."

No, you're doing what most people do, which is what?

"I'm not sure."

Not thinking about the pain. Do you think it is too painful to think about pain?

"Yes."

Why do you not want to think about it? Why don't people want to change? Why don't people think?

"It would be too painful."

It's an assumed pain. If you anticipate and deal with the possible repercussions of an event early on, by the time it occurs the emotional impact will not be as you predicted, and bearable nonetheless. However, if you do not anticipate your reaction to events, you may find yourself experiencing unexpected pain when they do occur.

Anticipating events and your reaction to them can help you adjust your energy to what will transpire. It also allows you to draw in more than what would normally be there. By anticipating and thinking about an event, you will experience a different kind of learning. Down the road, by the time this book is published, you may want to write your own book and say to yourself, "That information I learned from doing the Seth book is nothing; wait until you get a hold of mine." Do you understand me?

"Yes."

It is important to think about what is coming. This does not mean you should live in the future, but to think about the future. In this moment, you are living your future because, in the future, this moment will be a reflection of it. This moment is a creation of what will occur in two years time or in five years time. Whatever you do now is an aspect of five years down the road. Does this make sense? Are you not everything in this moment that you will be in five years time?

"Yes."

Yes, it is important to consider your reality in five years and more importantly to consider the present. If you make the choice to understand your present reality, then in five years you won't be scrambling in an unknown reality, something that is unexplained, not understandable.

Your thoughts can take you into unchartered waters. For instance, you can, in a sense, alter your future by anticipating your reaction to future events. By thinking about what could happen, how you will feel, why you will feel it, what you can and cannot change, and how you will deal with those feelings, you will meet the future without fear. You will know that you are safe.

What I think will happen may or may not occur, but by 'thinking' and considering all the angles you will feel safe and find no reason for fear or anxiety. By anticipating your destiny and also considering your current reality, you will discover possibilities you never considered before. For instance, you might find that you could write a book, and in thinking this, you will manifest this new reality and actually make it happen simply because you have focused on it.

If you do not do the work, events may unfold differently. You may not discover the possibility of writing your own book or your true desires. Your thinking has a way of helping you to achieve different realities. Your thoughts give you the information to help you physically manifest other realities.

When you ask yourself why you are afraid, why you are upset, why you think you're inadequate and why you think you have lost, you will learn that these thoughts are unimportant.

You need to ask yourself these hard core questions and from there, you can begin to investigate different realities. Different realities are just different thoughts, and different thoughts lead to different choices. Through choice, you can decide where it is you need to go.

"This is fascinating."

I do hope that I don't get this soul, Dale Landry, into trouble for talking about this, but again it is only my perception through his reality, not anything that necessarily has to be valid or true. It is just a perception, through his perception, through his reality, that was an unknown reality, an unknown thought at one time.

I am delighted once again to have had this opportunity to speak with you. As a reflection of you, I know that my desire would be for this session to go on and on and on, and ironically, it will.

Until I have the opportunity to be at your door once again and until we shall discover the truth within, may God and the universe speed you towards the light that you have always been and always will be.

"Thank you."

Seth was more passionate in his dictation this evening, and once again, he opened up areas within myself that I never imagined before. I was already anticipating my evening adventure. There is an unknown reality for me to experience and I could feel both the excitement and fear building up inside.

ᔕESSION 10ᴀ

GOD

Tuesday, May 19, 1998 - Over the weekend, I sat with my mother and asked her the questions I had hoped to have answered.

Ironically, I discovered both nothing and everything about myself through my conversation with her. In other words, I could see that she didn't have the answers I wanted even though I originally thought she would. There were times in our discussion where I could see her bewilderment and confusion, and I felt badly that I was torturing her. I was unaware of the impact I was having on her and was only concerned with my need for answers to my problems. Walking away from our conversation, I felt like a hunter who had shot his first deer, elated at the kill, yet unfulfilled inwardly, knowing that the hunt was not yet over.

This was perhaps a turning point for me to see that the answers to my questions would not come easily and a part of me needed to learn to forgive myself for what I felt I had missed in life. In so doing, I would be able to not just forgive my mother as I needed to but also release those issues around my mother that I needed to release. Thinking about these things, I understood how writers, artists and other creative types can be so tortured by their past, for mine was beginning to haunt me more than ever.

I arrived this evening to find only Dale at home. After getting a cup of coffee, our fuel for each session, we were ready for Seth to begin.

75

When I speak of God, I speak of my own thoughts, ideas and expressions around the term God. I am not speaking about the Bible nor should what I say change your personal perception of God. I am simply expressing what God means to me in my creative process. Do not misinterpret what I am describing as a threat to your God or your perception of God.

For many, their image of God changes as they grow and mature, and by the end of one's life, a person's perception of God is usually of gentleness and benevolence. This is not to say that young people don't believe in a loving God, but that only in later years do people see God as both a kinder and greater being.

This universe created itself about thirty billion years ago, much more than just the earth and the other eight planets. The earth developed much later although it is a component of the universe that was created originally. What is now the planet earth was originally a part of another galaxy and another planet within this universe. Earth is constantly moving through space and time, not only within its current orbit around the sun, but also at another time outside its orbit. Within the universe, the earth is like a particle of dust that travels as the wind and gravity push and pull it, sometimes great distances and sometimes none at all.

When the universe created itself, there was an explosion of thought that in turn created life. Life expanded and grew in many different forms at the original place where earth began, and was inhabited with both non-physical life forms and other creations you would consider human. Each person is a thought form covered in a coating we know as the physical body. The original planet where earth existed was not inhabited by physical life. It was only after earth broke away from another galaxy to the current universe that life began to physically manifest. Life as you know it is energy and movement and within this energy is a core of thought. This thought creates and propels energy, and the energy in turn manifests itself into physical forms such as rocks, plants, animals and humans. The planet is made up of energy of differing vibrations that are contained within each part of a rock, a plant, an animal and humans. Life forms that you believe to be 'alien' are vibrations that seek to inhabit earth but are not from your planet.

God is manifested as a complex thought form. The Gestalt combustion or the 'self-creating prophecy' of this universe is but one small particle of an even greater dimension of thought that goes beyond what you can possibly conceive of. In the future, you will want to know and come to understand more about this complex thought form. Because you exist in a physical world, it is difficult for you to conceive that your thoughts can travel billions of miles in seconds.

In this universe and beyond, travelling in thought takes only a moment since all time exists simultaneously. Your thoughts can actually travel three billion miles, but you cannot conceive this since you have chosen to root your current thoughts in a physical vibration to help you understand your existence. You can use, however, these thoughts to unleash the many unknown possibilities in your physical reality. As I have already stated, time is simultaneous and I can say that you have already travelled in space, in another reality and in another life. However, your thoughts will not permit you to see beyond, into another time, another dimension or another place. Because time is simultaneous does not mean that there are not alternate lifetimes and realities. I realize that these ideas are confusing and difficult to understand.

What you see as time is not necessarily time at all. It is a molecule of thought that keeps you contained in a vacuum while you grow and develop. If you truly understand thought and that God is a part of this thought process, you can comprehend the essence of God and why God exists. As the creator of your physical vibration, God can manifest anything He or She desires. Therefore, it follows that all humans as a part of God, can draw on His or Her energy to manifest anything it is they desire, such as love, kindness, compassion, empathy, understanding or acceptance.

Your soul has chosen to exist here in this physical vibration called the earth, to slow its vibration, its energy and its thoughts. In so doing, you have more energy and momentum to create future lives and realities in which you will live. To understand God, look in a mirror and ask yourself where you come from and where you are going. You will learn that you come from yourself, you go to yourself and you are always a part of yourself. Imagine your physical form dissolving before the mirror with only your energy or your vibration remaining. Your thoughts and thought forms can continue to look into the mirror even if your physical body is not there since your energy will always exist. When you imagine no physical body, what is revealed is the self beyond the physical, where you attune your vibration and core essence with all that surrounds you. In this way, you become a part of everything you see. It is at this point that you will understand that the God you see is a part of you, an all-inclusive God.

When you remove God, you remove the self and deny who and what you are. But even if you deny God's existence in your thoughts, you can never completely detach yourself from who you are. You will always sense that you are part of a greater picture, regardless of what you are taught. Remember, the farther removed you are from the truth, the more pain you will experience. But pain is but an experience which allows for growth and insight and it is perhaps for this reason that your soul desires the pain.

In simple terms, God is a form of energy that encourages love, ideas and images. God creates a continuously evolving energy that both moves through time, yet stands still in the moment. You may not understand my perception of God, but with time and thought, you will begin to consider your existence more completely, such as what you produce, where you have evolved from and where your life journey will take you. God is also a journey and some believe that it is a journey homeward that is achieved in death. Death is another form of existence, simply without the physical body. Death is pure energy with thought.

For all that exists in your universe, the journey home ends when all aspects of the many different concepts, ideas and worlds come together as one and form that which was originally a thought beyond an idea. If five different universes beyond this one come together in time, there is an element of completion, of pieces joining, and this completion is a return to home. The initial purpose for creating human life was to provide growth, movement and creation that would 'come together as one'—to bring each of us home in the end.

There is incredible complexity to what I am explaining but as you learn to use your thoughts to propel your energy, the movement of your thoughts, objects and your physical body will become much easier. However, you must first understand that these changes are possible.

78

To understand how God created earth, you must understand that you have also played a role in creating it. Understand that everyone and everything that exists has created everyone and everything that exists. This is one aspect of God, but beyond the God I speak of is a greater God. Within the hierarchy of existence, there are different levels of God just as there are like different levels of your vibration on this physical plane. Thus, as you become more adept at moving your energy and thought, you will become more attuned to your vibration and the different frequencies and thoughts of the God vibration which is also called the universal light. Furthermore, you will see that growth and evolution requires movement, change, altitude and energy. What you see at the end of your journey will be very much different from what you see at the beginning—the view becomes increasingly more spectacular as you move upwards.

You do not need to find direction and purpose in your physical vibration to exist. You could stand motionless and still grow and achieve insight. Your world operates on limits of perception, in other words, you are limited by your perceptions and beliefs of what is possible. However, humankind is beginning to unveil its history, its roots, its direction and its purpose beyond your perceptions of this physical vibration. As a part of the collective, when you learn to truly engage your thoughts, move beyond this physical world to discover your destination, and realize that there is one continuous moment in time where time is neither spent nor lost, you will find greater gentleness, virtue and patience.

I asked Seth a question about a part of his dictation. He asked me to repeat my question, but before I could finish, he stopped me again.

Stop right now, in the moment. By sitting and listening, did you miss anything by not asking the question, and me not answering it?

"No."

You wanted to ask me a question, and I stopped you midway. So, have you missed anything by not expressing your question?

"No, I guess not."

Are you sure? You did not have the chance to ask the question. So, wasn't something missed when I didn't hear or answer it?

"Yes."

What was missed?

I didn't answer Seth's question. Now, I wasn't so sure anymore.

You missed only what you perceived to miss. If I am linked to you, I already know your answer, and if you are linked to me, you already know my answer. So your question has no purpose, only an assumed purpose, because it is a limited form of communication. Stand still in the moment, listen with your thoughts and energy and you will discover a new form of language. You will discover that there is no possibility for anything to be missed, only what you perceive to be missed. Do you understand fully what I'm saying?

"I believe I do."

If you spent your life in jail, would you miss life?

"No."

But you would perceive you had.

"Yes."

It would be your perception that something was being lost. Am I correct?

"Correct."

If there is no time, but only a perception of time, then the loss or the feeling of loss is only a perception and not a reality of what truly exists. Time is a perception. Life in jail is only a moment, even though it would seem to many like an eternity. It is a perception within a perception; a thought within a thought. If you have spent time in prison, but have been freed, are you still imprisoned?

"Probably."

I believe you are imprisoned if you perceive yourself to be a prisoner. You are imprisoned in your physical vibration, and the prisons your society builds are a reflection of your feelings of imprisonment in your physical vibration. Do you understand?

"Yes."

Your prisons, your society, your lives and your realities reflect and express the collective of all peoples' inner thoughts.

We continued on to the next session.

BEAUTY

M^{*ay 19, 1998 - (continued)*}

Over time, society has evolved, communication has expanded and standards of living have improved. And, as the standards of living have improved, so has the desire for physical beauty, which is mistakenly believed to be obtainable by monetary means. Physical beauty is highly valued in Western society, and for some, it offers the perception of status.

Clearly, people believe that physical beauty leads to a fulfilling life but this is only a perception. Therefore, you must first look beyond this myth and focus on the true beauty that resides within. People's desire for improved outward appearances is really a desire to express their inner beauty.

You deceive and limit yourself by rejecting the things in life you believe are unattractive. By shedding your desires for physical attractiveness, you eliminate your expectations of perfection and can allow your true essence or your soul to shine through. To focus on your inner beauty is to focus on the light that lies within all things you once saw as unattractive. You can then move beyond your past judgements of yourself and others.

You are limited in this physical reality by your beliefs, desires and thoughts. As an example, if you desire love, do not allow this desire itself to limit you. A desire for love is an expectation of love and this itself will hinder you from receiving it. If you desire love, visualize it and repeat the words, "I release this desire for love." Then, deliver this thought from your feelings. Each time you deliver this thought, you will express outwardly to the universe your request for love. This example can be used for anything else you desire.

Universal laws are stringent and therefore will not allow you to manifest love or anything else if you hold strings or have expectations. Love only exists in itself; it does not exist to set you free. Those individuals who have been touched by love, in this lifetime or another, know that there are no words to describe this emotion.

Love can transcend even your concept of God. It can move you beyond your physical vibration, and is a reflection of why thought and its expression was first created. Love is an explosion of thought and energy, and encompasses all in your physical world. It is both material and spiritual, and yet it is neither. It moves freely between all worlds and vibrations. You can desire and seek love, but do not expect it.

It is difficult to explain some of these ideas I speak of, however, what I say should have some sense of clarity and accuracy. All souls like you, living in this physical reality, have come to learn certain things, to understand their purpose and are reverting back to this phase of 'knowingness'. But, the changes you seek must be gradual. If change occurs too quickly, there would be much chaos. Change can happen in a moment, but it may take two billion years to reach that moment.

I am providing you with this information to show you a world beyond your limiting beliefs. There is much to be learned, and through your gifts, abilities and thoughts, you can achieve more than you thought was possible. The essence of this book is self expression and creativity which is a mirror of your inner core. But first, you must go back to the beginning and understand where it is you came from, and next recognize where you will go and witness the totality of your experience, all in the same moment.

When you read this material, you will see the truth in what I am saying. You will know that you have experienced what I am saying. The purpose of this book is to go beyond the limitations of what is expressed in your world.

If you know that there is purpose beyond death, you can understand that death is as much a beginning as an ending. All aspects of your existence, whether in this physical reality or in the metaphysical realm, are important for your soul's purpose.

I cannot accomplish my purpose without you. If you did not listen, I would not talk. You exist together and not separately. You may live as a separate entity from your neighbour, but all people in society still exist as one.

You may explain these thoughts to someone else, or you may take them and explain them in your own way. Each person's thoughts are a part of the self, a part of God and are an expression even beyond your understanding of God.

God is not a molecule inside your head which you visualize as a divine light. He/She is beyond your physical reality, beyond the spirit that lives after death. He/She is beyond your imagination, yet He/She is a part of you and everything in your universe. What is two billion miles away is also linked to you, both separate yet one with you. You can communicate with Him/Her, but you cannot speak to Him/Her.

I wish to discuss my views on poverty. What purpose would there be for people of means if poverty was eliminated? Would wealthy people be more content knowing they no longer had to share their wealth? Or, would they be saddened because a 'part' of them was eliminated?

"Saddened."

They would be neither. The poor would not be gone. The poor simply would be in an alternate vibration, still a part of and never separate from the 'wealthy'.

People of means believe that those who are poor are separate from themselves. But, they are not separate, they are one. If the poor are not fed, then the rich are neither. In other words, to withhold love and compassion, and ignore the suffering of another, is to deny a part of your self. All people in your physical reality and your physical vibration are one, a part of the whole. Your eventual purpose is to be responsible for one another. Until this feat is accomplished, neither yourself or anyone else can get beyond your limited reality.

The wealthy often believe that those who are poor have created their own reality. And, those who are poor often believe that they have sinned and that their poverty is their punishment. But, neither the poor nor the rich are being punished. Punishment is only a perception. Life is meant to be shared, and through sharing, you will discover freedom and a return to the 'oneness' that each of you are a part of.

Humanity's evolution is a process of learning and even those who lack great intellect and insight are a part of this evolutionary process. However, the life purpose of those who lack intellect and insight may not be to learn intellectually, but may be to learn through feelings and emotions.

What is lacking is the ability of people to go beyond their individual life purpose in this physical reality and see beyond. Society as we know it will continue to exist until each person achieves some level of change. If one person is imprisoned, all are imprisoned, and, in turn, your own God is imprisoned.

Even if I leave you without words, there is still an undeniably great deal of thought that links us for our mutual good.

When Dale came out of trance, we discussed the impact that Seth's information was having upon us. While Dale felt an immediate effect, I felt a deeper impact when I transcribed the tapes at home.

When I transcribed the tapes of each session at home, alone in my thoughts, there was a sense of freedom to explore and ponder these ideas more intensely.

Rick returned home as we were closing the session, and after discussing the details of our upcoming trip to Maine, I left to go home.

Into the evening, I took a break from my typing and turned on the television just in time to catch the end of a documentary which, ironically, was about Leonard Cohen, a personality Seth had spoken about in a previous session.

At this point, I reflected on the session I was transcribing and knew that the book was almost complete. This saddened me as I thought that soon Seth would say the last session was near.

SESSION 11

LOCKED IN TIME

Wednesday, May 20, 1998 - This evening when I arrived, Laura was on the Internet. I joined her at the computer and passed the time learning about 'surfing the net'.

When I met up with Dale to begin the night's session, we were delayed when we quickly discovered there were no blank tapes available for recording. Our search throughout the house failed to turn one up. Fortunately, Sarah came to our rescue and we were ready to resume.

You may question my relationship with Jane. It is difficult to explain why she channelled me. Jane Roberts was a very genuine and unique individual who loved life's finer things, but more importantly, she placed a high value on intellectual achievement. Jane also had a side to her that desired unusual things and her alternate lifestyle led her in the direction of channelling.

Some may feel that this individual I speak through, Dale Landry, has no right to speak about Jane. However, this 'Jane' I speak of may be one aspect of my own metaphysical reality that I created in your physical world, but who never truly existed. For all I know, she may still be channelling some other soul.

When you question your actions, you discover an array of possibilities to manifest your goals. My point is that thoughts are real and they may evoke desires to inspire you to achieve your goals.

To believe you exist as one thought is to believe you can only think in one dimension, but there are many dimensions to your thoughts and many realities or worlds that you can travel in and out of. Being tuned into one physical vibration does not prevent you from using many of the other frequencies and the other areas of your thoughts. Your thoughts are like antennae that can access other worlds and realities of thought.

For example, some 500 years ago, the soul of Nostradamus had visions of the modern-day airplane although he never saw an actual plane. It would be years after his death before the first airplane was flown, but this example shows it is possible for your thoughts to become a physical reality.

As I have previously stated, time is simultaneous and therefore it does not exist. You may have a thought or a desire in one physical reality, where it is never fully achieved. Yet, you follow through with this thought or desire in another life. For example, you may desire to become a concert pianist in one life, but never achieve this goal. However, in another physical reality, you already are a pianist.

While Nostradamus prophesied a plane during one life, is it not possible that he existed, simultaneously, in another life, to actually help develop the airplane? Perhaps, he was subconsciously aware of this 500 years ago because he was linked in thought to the life wherein he developed the plane, and therefore, could see it.

Everything happens in the here and now. Your physical reality is the totality of all of your thoughts, so your thoughts are your physical reality. As you think and create thoughts, you create your physical reality. To make the proverbial statement, "You think, therefore you are."

Suppose that God does not exist. Without God, is there a reality? God is a part of all of your many lifetimes. If you can understand that idea in this life and your other lives occur simultaneously, you will understand how all souls overlap, yet are linked as one. To use a basic example, Tom in this lifetime was Susan in another. Yet, in this lifetime, Tom's best friend is Susan.

I know it is complex and difficult to comprehend. Time travel does not exist. It is only an illusion that you are moving forward. Do you think you'll be free? What will you be free from? From pain, work or stress? What is freedom? Freedom is only a thought. Does it make sense to seek freedom in this lifetime when you were not free in another? Each of your realities work to change the other, including the future and the past. But with no past and no future, all reality occurs in one moment.

Some may find it hard to understand how they can change their past, but let us look at an example. One who was not liked in school, for whatever the reason, could now learn to like himself or herself, and at another time in the future, you will come to a point where you actually will like yourself. When you achieve the ability to like yourself, immediately, your assumed past will change and those who once did not like you will take on a different opinion. You changed your reality through your thoughts. All of this thinking was simultaneous despite the many different realities and thoughts you had in one moment. You linked them together to create a reality in which you now like yourself. In other words, you created a reality where you didn't like yourself and a reality where you did, and joined the two thoughts together. The result was to resolve the idea that, even though the students from school are no longer in your life, they had liked you in the past.

I will present another example. Suppose, the soul I am speaking through, Dale Landry, put on a pair of rubber gloves and then two minutes later took them off. Was one life lived with both gloves on, and one without? Each moment is a reality, and in each moment you create a thought that has a life of its own. As one moment passes, you move into a different reality and another thought. All thoughts occur simultaneously and exist as a reality unto themselves.

There are so many different realities and so many different lifetimes you are not consciously aware of. But if you look closely at the possibility that other realities do exist, you will see sides of yourselves that you never knew existed before.

Is this making sense to you?

"Yes."

I will end here. It is difficult to explain alternate realities and simultaneous lifetimes to the many who have been taught to think in only one way. My point in giving you this information is to change your linear thinking and to propose the idea that there are other realities than just the one you see. By moving beyond your linear thinking, you can start to see life for what it is, not what you expect it to be.

If you move through this lifetime constantly depressed, you may assume that you are depressed for many reasons. But could your depression stem from events that occurred in another reality?

Look at the history of war. What problems did war itself solve? None, except perhaps for a short term change in which one group dominated over another. Your religious doctrine is to love one another, yet your history books are filled with details of the many wars waged for the love of God. If these wars are a reflection of you and your realities, your realities and lifetimes are painful existences. So, how will you learn to right the wrongs of your alternate realities?

The key is to open yourself up to your thoughts. If you accomplish this challenge, you will discover riches beyond your wildest dreams, and if you learn to open up your thoughts and then to express them, you will find compassion and kindness that you never knew existed. Aspire to be who you are, in the moment, and not what you think you should be. If you are not happy with yourself, and do not love yourself, accept that pain and understand that it is a part of who you are. Discover the riches that exist within.

It was a joy to have had this opportunity to be in your physical reality, even if it isn't a reality but a thought. Until I shall appear in your thoughts again, much joy, happiness and inspiration.

It's certainly difficult to embellish on what Seth has spoken of, but it does leave me with a lot to think about.

WHO'S ON TOP

Thursday, May 12, 1998 - After only a brief hello to Laura, we were ready to start our session on time.

What I want to discuss today may be somewhat humorous to some but it has a very serious undertone.

If you are a heterosexual man and had the opportunity to become a woman, would you make the switch? If yes, why and what would be the advantage? And if no, why not? If given the chance, a woman would more easily make the switch to becoming a man which shows me the bias and prejudice that still exist in your society.

This discussion tonight may be somewhat confusing, so bear with me. To generalize, if a man took the role of a woman, he would be perceived as vulnerable and weak. In becoming a woman, a man's first desire would not be to understand a woman's mind and thoughts, but also to have big breasts, a beautiful body and a pretty face. Men often think that these attributes are what women themselves desire, but this is not true.

Women want to be attractive, but throughout history, this is how men have always wanted women to be. Essentially, women want to appeal to men, they don't necessarily want these attributes for themselves. If a women took on a man's mind and thoughts, she would also take on his personality and his intelligence, but not his physical looks. A man's appearance is not considered a priority to most women.

I could feel that Seth was really enjoying this session. He broke out into laughter many times.

Men believe that having an attractive woman at their side offers prestige and credibility. However, a beautiful and intelligent woman could make him look insignificant and not in control. Men who choose to be with intelligent women often see themselves as social outcasts.

The other reason that men want women with large breasts and beauty is to fulfill their sexual fantasies. Sexual thoughts are common among men and they are often transfixed on a woman's anatomy. So, what a man would desire as a woman is enjoying continuous sexual stimulation.

Seth started to laugh again here.

However, I'm not quite sure if a man would find true satisfaction having sex as a woman. While the sex would fulfill his many desires, he would also discover how unattentive a man is to a woman's sexual needs. Men are generally focused on themselves during sex. If women treated men as men treated women during sex, men would strongly reconsider their position in society and in sex. Thus, to sense a woman's sexual needs, it is crucial for men to put themselves in a woman's position.

In turn, women have allowed themselves to be oppressed, but the onus is on them to find sexual equality. Therefore, when women own up to and take responsibility for their intellectual abilities, men will accept the true essence of women. Ironically, women see men as intellectually replete because men often fall prey to female manipulation.

Turning to women, suppose that women could become men, what would they do first? What would you choose first, Christine, if you were a man? Would you want power or status?

"Good question."

You mean you never thought about it?

"Not in depth. . . I'd choose power."

I agree. On a subconscious level, women would desire men's power rather than their sexual superiority. Clearly, men and women look at life differently. In many ways, women see themselves as insignificant to men and many believe that men hold the key to power. What women do not see is that they give up their power to men; they give up their independence, their intelligence and play a secondary role. These thoughts have arisen from history's beliefs about the role of men and women. In this discussion, however, I do not suggest that women take over. Simply put, women have a vulnerable energy and men have a dominant one, but being dominant does not mean that they have ownership. This is obviously a generalization, however, dominance is an aggressive initiating force, while vulnerability is a passive, receiving energy. There are many women who have an aggressive, initiating energy and there are men who are vulnerable and receiving.

To equalize the balance of power, society must relinquish its limiting myths and contradictions. To do so, each gender must consider the advantages and disadvantages of living as the opposite sex.

Each person, be it a man or a woman, has both a male and female side. However, men are not encouraged to develop their feminine 'emotional' side, and women not their male 'intellectual' side. To do so would produce strong criticism and judgement.

Some may use my ideas to argue that women should dominate men. However, this discussion is about each gender learning to express all parts of themselves, and both men and women together need compassion, strength and understanding.

As far as relationships are concerned, there is a common myth which stems from centuries of religious conditioning that God can provide anyone with a relationship. But nothing could be further from the truth. You choose to create a relationship, and ultimately, you will learn from it. No relationship is perfect; they each have their difficulties. But as you learn responsibility, gain insight and grow with it, you will also learn forgiveness, compassion and how to create an environment that will benefit you and your partner.

People first learn about relationships from their parents. Your idea of relationships is based on your parent's relationship, but it is likely your parents had little understanding of a successful relationship themselves.

Often, the preceding generation entered into relationships for survival, or material or social successes. These values have been passed onto you. Now, you must adopt a new perspective in order to find success in a relationship.

Try to imagine living as the other sex to understand 'the other side's' sense of value. For instance, how does it feel when your male partner controls you? Do you enjoy being manipulated by your female partner? In same sex relationships, how can two men be together if they can't commit? How can two women move beyond their misguided desire to nurture? In all relationships, it will appear that something is lacking, but it is up to you to find out what it is, and to look deep within to discover what is missing.

A relationship can help you to express your inner self. Finding a relationship that offers security and acceptance will provide a sense of recognition and completion from your partner. If you can see your importance and find your true self, you will feel supported and recognize that nobody can bring you down. You will also be accepted and recognized by your peers.

There are some who do not desire a relationship, but the painful part of not having one is that society believes you are worthless without one. This belief originated in a time when women were considered the property of men and men were obligated to protect them, though they were anything but protected.

So why does a society which values independence not eliminate its age old beliefs and incorporate new ideas, ones that benefit everyone?

I do not feel the need to discuss race or interracial relationships. In my eyes, there are only men and women, and thus, no distinction of race. On an intuitive level, each individual, regardless of his or her ignorance or conditioning, knows there is no distinction between the races except the difference a person creates. And so, each problem, hardship or difficulty you create is a reflection of you.

If you are willing to change and see beyond what you have been conditioned to believe, you will understand the beauty and essence of simply being human—not male, not female, just human. Therefore, when you acknowledge and accept your human side, you will develop compassion for others and yourself, and you will also know how precious life is. You must experience the quiet moments, and periods of boredom, to reflect on the thoughts that reveal your inner self and to acknowledge the parts you like and dislike. To acknowledge these parts can at first be quite painful, but in the end, it is enjoyable. The result of this work on the 'self' is a sense of security and knowing your inner being. My purpose is to help you discover your own expression of independence and the direction you want to create in your life. Using your relationships to create and express these discoveries is as important as anything else you do.

Until I have the opportunity to speak with you again, may God speed you towards the moment, to the light, to the love that is ever present in you, and may you recognize your value well beyond your years.

I was amazed and intrigued at how Seth was able to portray the views of men and women from a similar, yet very different perspective. It gave me a good deal of insight into how I needed to see men differently. I find that in doing these sessions with Seth, he is a constant challenge to my thought process and at times he leaves me feeling like there was so much more I could have done in the past, and a great deal more I need to do in future.

This session was shorter, but certainly very powerful.

DELIVERANCE

*F*riday, May 22, 1998 - No one was at Dale's home when I arrived but I knew Dale wouldn't be far behind. I had always arrived at our scheduled time and Dale always poked fun at my promptness.

On one level, I admired his ability to be so laid back and at ease. At the same time, I couldn't help but feel that I was being taken a bit for granted. It was at times like this that I was happy I smoked.

I waited no more than a minute until I saw Dale and Corinne walking up the street. We started the session shortly after getting a coffee.

If a couple marries at age eighteen or twenty, and after ten or fifteen years, and two children, realize they are unhappy in their relationship, should they divorce or separate?

"Would this be a decision after having tried to work out their relationship together?"

I am asking you the question. What do you think?

"Okay, they should separate or divorce."

What does society tell you they should do?

"Stay together."

When a couple separates, what do both experience? Let's take the male first. What do you assume a male goes through?

"I believe he would go through an emotional period first and then be much quicker to carry on with his life than the woman."

What would the woman go through?

"Compared to the man, the woman would probably experience ten times the emotional stress, simply because she has the children and probably would need to start all over again."

Both would experience an equal amount of pain but society tells you differently. Society tells you that the man would rebound much more quickly and find another relationship. At the same time, society says that the woman would fall into a rut believing herself to be worthless. Women accept this belief and often have difficulty recovering from a failed relationship, but what most people do not notice is that while the man may appear to have rebounded quicker, his devastation from the separation is not over. Both the man and the woman will experience the same pain and require an equal amount of time to recover. However, if the couple had strong communication skills during the marriage, then an amicable separation is possible.

It is still believed that men are dominant in society and sometimes are more valued than women. Women accept this idea and believe it is difficult to attract a man, often engaging in a relationship with any man who chooses them. This belief results from a desperate need to be loved, and, from this desperation, men have a greater choice of women with low self esteem. When a woman rejects this belief and values herself, she will attract a man who will also provide integrity, equality and support.

Especially in North American society, people in general are 'needy' and co-dependent. For instance, women marry men under the guise that it is better to have any man than no man at all. Making a poor choice will ultimately lead to inner turmoil, pain, and confusion. It can take as much as twenty years before one realizes that the suffering in a relationship is needless and unnecessary. However, to leave a painful relationship creates feelings of tremendous guilt, a lack of self worth and a sense of failure. Under these circumstances, a separation or divorce may seem impossible.

To generalize once again, men do not seek marriage only for the sake of marrying. Men believe that there will always be opportunities for marriage, and marry for status, enjoyment and sex, but never because it is the 'right' thing to do. And like a woman, fifteen or twenty years into an unsatisfactory relationship, a man will also realize that his partner does not fulfill his emotional needs.

Men and women often blame each other for their difficulties. Women do not discover their true value and may feel desperate for a relationship, and men do not attune themselves to their emotional needs or properly assess the relationships they enter into. So, Christine, what is the solution?

"To go within the self."

It is easy to offer the 'self' as a solution, but finding the answer is quite difficult.

How do you get the message to those who do not listen? How do you tell a woman to nurture and love herself first, and create the circumstances to make her whole? How do you tell a man to develop his feelings when most are emotionally distant?

I related this thought to my own experience and realized I needed help with my feelings of low self-esteem. As a result, I made a choice to seek a number of alternatives to improve myself.

Coming back to relationships, why start one if you don't really want it? Why pretend? Why spend thirty or forty years proving to your neighbours that you are worthy because you have married the right man or woman? You only end up squandering your life away.

People will go to counsellors to understand what is wrong with them and why they cannot have a relationship. But the simple explanation is that society tells people that something is wrong with them if they cannot find a relationship. You and everyone else are unique, each with unique desires, but society embraces the status quo, not what is considered 'unique'.

Turning to another example, at one time centuries ago if someone was sick or in need of shelter, he or she was offered assistance. But in this moment those who are sick and those who are homeless are kept at a distance; they are often seen as dirty and unwanted.

It is not my goal to preach. I am simply showing you what society expects of you. If you pretend to be something you are not, it will cause much unnecessary pain. Similarly, if you recognize that people who are homeless are very much a part of you, why do you continue to ignore them?

Society and the community at large must pull together. People must learn to trust, assist and support one another. Through this effort, you will discover what it is you need to do.

There is no need for homelessness or sickness in your society. If you supported and worked with each other, these issues would not exist. Unfortunately, people believe that to achieve success their needs must come first. These needs, however, blind people and leave them as homeless as those who live on the street.

Many people pretend to be happy but live in an empty shell, isolated from their family and the people close to them. Happiness is just an illusion people try to create.

In truth, approximately seventy percent of people in Western society claim they are unhappy and unsatisfied in their marriages, whether or not there are children. Clearly, many have made the same mistakes as their parents. They have had children because they believed their purpose was to procreate. But this is a false belief, perpetuated by society and religious doctrine.

The world is incredibly overpopulated, but no one takes notice. People do not educate themselves and don't listen. How unhealthy must the world get before people realize the extent of their problems? As the death toll rises into the year 2000 and beyond, will you assume that those who are dying are being punished? This is precisely what society and religious leaders will tell you. Or, will you believe that for those who pass away, it is simply their time to go, or will you become frightened that you could be next?

What I say may appear harsh and critical, but take heed, it is neither. As a soul who delivers this information, I only provide a message to those who choose to hear it. Ultimately, each person will discover for themselves whether the message is appropriate. My words are not gospel, but ask yourself whether the message fits for you.

The world will be a much better place when men are willing to explore their female side and learn to be more sensitive and emotional, while women must discover their true value and take responsibility for themselves. Look closely at yourself and deal with your issues. Remember that you and your partner are at your best behaviour at the start of a new relationship. It is only later on, once you have made a long-term commitment, that the less attractive side shows through. Then you can see whether you married someone you don't really know or married someone who simply mirrors the traits you deny in yourself.

I leave you with this final thought—if you were a child of God and God appeared before you one day, would you recognize Him/Her? More importantly, would you recognize God if you had never seen Him/Her?

Do you have any answers for this, Christine?

"No I don't." *I tried to elaborate further on my response but I was confused.*

You said no, but then went on to give a jumbled answer. Why is that? Are you afraid of being wrong?

"Yes."

Are you afraid that I will judge you for being wrong? Will that make you less in my eyes?

"Maybe. Yes, I am embarrassed when I give the wrong answer."

What is it you fear in being wrong.

I didn't answer.

What part of your parents do I mirror back to you? The disciplinarian? The part that needs perfection? The part that believes you are not doing well enough at school?

"I'd have to say all of them."

If you knew that consciously, would you still have answered "no" to my first question about God?

"I might have told you what I truly believed."

And you knew the answer?

I remained silent and close to tears at this point.

It was somewhat of a trick question, but nevertheless, you do understand what I am saying?

"I think so."

You know what you need to know, but you deny your awareness of this knowledge. If you were attuned to your energy and awareness, you wouldn't fear the question because you would know my purpose in asking it. You answered the question from the perspective that I was rating your performance, which is how your parents would have asked the question and probably how you would have responded. What they would have wanted to know is if my daughter intelligent or ignorant? Will she get the question right or fail? Do you see what I am saying?

"Yes, I do."

The answer to my question of whether you would recognize God is that you would know Him/Her because you are a part of Him/Her. So if you choose a relationship, choose it from the perspective that you know what is best for you, not what you think is best.

Imagine that we are best friends and that we grew up and spent most of our lives together, but I always thought that you were more beautiful than me. As the years went by, I believed that your beauty became more radiant and I seethed with jealousy to the point where I could no longer tolerate it. As a result, our friendship ended. Who would feel more pain, you at having lost your best friend or me at having given up my best friend?

"You for having given up your best friend."

Interesting. I would have said you.

"Why me?"

You would be more pained because you are as much a culprit with your beauty as I am. You let me believe that you were more beautiful instead of telling me I was as beautiful as you.

Pain is an illusion and regardless of who gave up on the relationship, my pain would be a reflection of yours. In essence, we mirror each other's pain, and whoever you draw into your life, he or she may help you to grow but would still mirror your emotional desires, needs and wants. You may believe your friends are not as beautiful or intelligent simply because they mirror the ugliness and stupidity that resides within you. The true extent of a person's intelligence, knowledge and wisdom is relative to who is looking in the mirror.

One last question. If you were a man and discovered your wife of twenty years was cheating on you, would you confront her?

"Yes, I would."

I guess, either way, she has to live with her deception.

"Yes."

So why bother wasting your energy? Doesn't one learn by example? Why do you need to confront her with a deception you already know about? If she is cheating, why do you need to express it? And if you already know what has occurred, are you not responsible for your own actions?

"I would have to decide whether I wanted to stay or go."

Not quite. You would need to ask yourself whether you still loved her. If you did, you would need to deal with things and get on with your life. If you didn't, then you could decide to do whatever it is you had to do. More importantly, if you didn't love your wife, you shouldn't be in the relationship in the first place. Do you agree?

"Yes. It makes a lot of sense."

Why is your society so torn and tattered because of extra marital affairs?

"I assume it is because of society and religion."

And their beliefs? Let others be responsible for their own decisions and choices and you make your own choices based on where you are, not based on where you are emotionally and spiritually. Do not make choices based on other's ideas.

The reason I asked you take a man's perspective on his unfaithful wife is because in your society it is more acceptable for a man to stray from his marriage than it is for a woman. Women are taught to accept an unfaithful husband because it is "natural" for men to be unfaithful. In reality, it is not "natural" for men to cheat, even though society believes it is acceptable. It is also a belief that women are conditioned to accept men's infidelity as a reality, but this is no more a reality for men as it is for women. It is the belief of two people to decide which direction their relationship must take.

I do not look to shift the balance of power, but to equalize it so that all individuals can find more joy in their lives. If only one group holds the power, everyone suffers.

"We have a long way to go."

I would prefer to say that you have come a long way, yet there is still much distance to travel for society to get to the moment.

I will end here. I believe that we covered the necessary territory for today's session. I am assuming that we are joining forces again tomorrow.

"Yes."

Any discoveries when you are transcribing the sessions?

"Yes, a tremendous amount. I'm finding that there is still a lot more to learn."

Is it easy to execute the information?

"What do you mean?"

Is it easy to implement it into your life?

As I was thinking of a response, Seth continued.

You didn't answer my question. I suppose that will be a part of what we will talk about tomorrow. 'Executing the Will' and answering questions directly.

"Thank you for today."

Until we have a moment together again, may God speed you towards the moment and to the realization of who you are and what you desire to achieve.

"Thank you."

This was an extremely emotional session for me. About midway through my throat began to tighten and I was holding back tears. Over the past several years, the more I discovered about myself, the more I seemed to want to hide it. What I perceived as a very ugly side to myself became unacceptable to me and I knew that if it was unacceptable to me, it would be unacceptable to whomever I was with.

When Dale came out of trance, I was in tears and having quite a time getting any words out. Dale has a tremendous amount of compassion and I was grateful for his caring nature and intuitive wisdom as he helped me through this difficult moment.

It is strange to read these notes again. I can see more clearly now how I had everything backwards, for if I had only accepted myself, I would not have felt the need to look to others for acceptance.

FAMILY OF THOUGHT

Tuesday, May 26, 1998 to Tuesday, June 2, 1998 - Our trip to Maine turned out very well. Dale's family owns a cottage there and we stayed there for one week. Due to work commitments, we all departed within days of each other. Dale drove down on a Tuesday with room mates Sarah and Rick, and friends David and Corinne. Rosaria, another friend, and myself drove down the next morning.

The unusually warm weather continued throughout our stay. We pursued activities such as swimming, nude sunbathing, reading, shopping, eating, playing board games, and socializing in the evening which made our holiday a complete success.

David and Corinne are fabulous cooks and we ate exceptionally well.

I found this trip to be more relaxing than my first time to Maine two years ago, maybe because I have grown to know everybody and feel quite comfortable with them.

Although Dale and I weren't working on the book, we still continued to be in sync with each other. On one occasion, as we sat listening to an "Oldies" station on the radio, with the songs from the sixties and seventies, we both experienced the same feeling that we were hearing the lyrics to songs we knew for the first time. Other times, as we were being impressed with our own revelations from the book, we would seek each other's company to share in our discoveries.

Seth's book was a huge part of our lives now, and for the few who could stay awake until the wee hours of the morning we sat and enjoyed our enlightening conversations together.

The world news for the week was filled with headlines of nuclear testing in Pakistan and India, tornado warnings in Toronto, a train derailment in Germany and a huge earthquake in Afghanistan.

Wednesday, June 3, 1998 - When I arrived this evening, Dale and Rick were out in the back yard taking it easy and waiting for the oven timer to go off. This afternoon Dale was inspired to bake bread, so as we continued to wait together, we laughingly wondered how baking bread might parallel our session in any way.

Once the bread was finished, we were ready to begin the session.

Now, I shall speak about the family. It is not the 'family' as you see it, but a family of thought that resides within each person.

Within your mind, your arms and your legs live a family of thoughts. Each thought is built upon the other. Your legs could function if you lost your arms, however, it would be difficult since both systems of thought move in unison. Your thought system, your whole family of thought, encompasses the mind and sends messages throughout your body. But each body part also has its own thought system, its own manner of approaching life, and each can function altogether independently.

The body of a healthy infant grows in unison, no one part growing more rapidly than the other. The head does not grow faster than the other parts, and as complex as this may sound, it is understandable that the rest of the body has its own functions and its own thought system.

Each part of the body plays a role in helping the mind and its thought system to operate. Together each part works as part of the whole, with one purpose. The mind is the first place for the body to manifest its thoughts.

People do not concentrate on individual body parts but focus on their mind and their body as a whole. If you concentrated on individual parts of your body you would be surprised at how each area responds to your attention. For example, if you take the time to nurture your legs, massage them and focus on them every day, you will find a great improvement in their energy and circulation. The thought system within the legs will respond to your attention, much like you would respond to the loving attention of another person. The system of thought that exists within the body is an intricate part of how you function. If some parts are neglected, the system of thought cannot work as a whole. Each part needs equal attention to operate properly. Neglected parts of the body will eventually break down or become unhealthy. To care for your body parts separately as part of the whole is a key element in learning to love yourself.

To create a solid marriage, it is imperative that both partners communicate with one another. If communication breaks down, disharmony, pain and the inevitable dissolution of the marriage may occur. Your body's thought system operates in much the same way. If you perform certain physical activities, you subconsciously or consciously give your body attention, letting it know that it needs to work well for the whole body to properly exist and function.

Some believe that certain physical activities may harm the body. But it is not the physical activity that causes harm, just a belief that harm and pain can create disharmony in the body. If you do not believe your body will age, it will not. To incorporate this belief, however, you must first understand how the universe and your physical reality functions. As you progress into the information age or the Age of Aquarius, over the next 1,000 years, you will be inundated with ideas on how to improve your health, your beauty and your lifestyle. But there will be little explanation on how to incorporate these changes into your life and into your belief system, although there will be descriptions on how to perform specific exercises.

To focus briefly on your emotional wellbeing, you may have read before that to improve your self-esteem you should look into a mirror each night and tell yourself you are beautiful. Eventually, the subconscious mind will adopt this belief and you will see yourself the way you want to be. But what is not fully explained is that through the boredom of repetition, it is unlikely you will maintain this activity for any length of time. To achieve success with this exercise, you must perform it numerous times to eventually accept and believe that you are beautiful and can stay young. Beauty and youth are one and the same. Believing you are beautiful allows you to grow old and mature, and still see your eternal beauty and youth deep within your soul.

To accept the challenge of bettering your lifestyle and physical wellbeing is an all consuming exercise. You cannot expect to stay young and beautiful if you do not focus your energy on making it happen. You must completely consume your efforts into this part of your life. It is possible to have youth, beauty, a loving relationship and material wealth all at once, but it is not likely with the beliefs you have now.

Society is consumed by the need to express itself as an entity; this will always exist. However, to step out of this need for social expression and back into your 'self', requires you to ask yourself whether your own personal desire to express yourself is more important than society's. Society believes that relationships are all-important, and does not allow you to believe you can be alone to enjoy your own experiences. This belief of society perpetuates the ongoing need of many to be accepted by the whole. If one leg is neglected it will respond with poor circulation and pain. You may believe you can have it all, but your religion, your parents, your friends and your society tells you that you cannot. It takes great strength to step away from society's belief system and incorporate your own, even if you believe you can.

At this point, I developed a tickle in my throat and started coughing intermittently during Seth's dictation. Obviously, this material was hitting home.

Your community is beginning to change and people are discovering their individuality, but many still feel neglected in their need to be loved. You are capable of giving yourself the attention and love you need, but you must adopt this new belief into your thinking before it can become a reality. Your body must change and adapt to this new awareness. Believing you can grow hair when you are bald is difficult when society says there is no cure for baldness. Thus, if you tell me that you are capable of change and I say you are not, does that support you in your effort to change or does it deter you from your growth? It would seem that the latter fits and you would have difficulty proving to me otherwise.

At this moment, your belief system is not one that is encouraging or supportive. People's background and upbringing lead them to develop strict and limiting beliefs about what is possible.

"So, Christine, is there a difficulty with how this is sitting with you?"

"I wonder, since I seem to have a tickle in my throat."

I couldn't explain the onset of my coughing spell but it would not let up during the remainder of the dictation. I kept trying to suppress the urge to cough as to not interrupt the session, but it wasn't easy.

Those raised in poverty may find the pursuit of financial prosperity and intellectual wealth impossible unless they are introduced, at some point, to the competitive world and develop the skills to conquer it.

You are moving away from an awareness of the 'self' and more into denial. Self-awareness allows you to independently determine what is best for you in your life. Denying the self keeps you in the dark and afraid, unable to make change or believe in choice. Those who deny who they are seek others who agree with their outlook; there is safety in numbers. Those who want to change, however, look for self-awareness and individuality, but are often persecuted by society. Nevertheless, the revolution of the self has begun and there is no stopping it. For each person who desires change, two people will not. In physical death you will find that life continues, that the voice within that cries out to discover who you are and your purpose is the voice that will always be with you, wherever and however you exist.

To deny a part of your 'self', whether in your mind or your body, is indeed a painful existence. Similarly, to imprison the one who speaks the truth is to confine yourself and others to a life of ignorance.

Ask yourself "Am I capable of change?" And if the answer is "No", say, "Yes, I can." If you question whether you can change, you have already decided to restrain your effort to do it. However, to know that you can change is to know you are changing.

Some believe that whatever will be will be; que sera, sera. So, yes, whatever will be will be, for what you have chosen it to be.

There are many things to understand that make change possible. In seeking youth, you will find that it is possible to obtain youth, physically, mentally, emotionally and spiritually. Thus, when you seek it, ask yourself what it will provide for you. If it can provide the many wondrous things that will bring you strength, a full life and contentment, then manifest it, but if your quest for youth is merely to build your ego, then shy away from it. If you cannot distinguish between what is ego and contentment, then your purpose in life may be to then understand this difference.

A dialogue then ensued between Seth and myself.

In your youth I believe you always had problems with your baby toe? Do you recall this?

"No, I believe my problems were with my breathing. I used to cough, just like I'm doing now, always at bedtime, disturbing everyone near me. I do remember that."

I found it curious and a little ironic that I grew up just a block from where Dale currently lives.

And so you got the attention you were not getting otherwise?

"Well, yes."

I'm sure that thought wasn't consciously going through my mind at the time.

Therefore, one part of your thought system was the need to be recognized and it manifested through your coughing. You created a negative situation to get positive reinforcement in order to know you were accepted, or recognized and loved.

"I agree."

What do you believe was causing your coughing today during our session?

"I'm not sure."

Seth rephrased the question.

How have you been challenged?

"To change."

To change how?

"To change my belief systems. To change the way I think."

Assuming your body was reacting to the information being delivered, I can only assume that it has already started responding to 'change' on a subconscious level, and has begun the process of adjusting to these changes.

"I'm glad to hear that."

Do not judge it. Simply recognize and accept it for what it is, not for what you want it to be. If change comes to you because it is good, what happens if there is no change? Is the rest of your life bad?

"I see what you are saying."

If I come to you without judgment, if I come to you as a soul who expresses creativity of thought, and you, in turn, accept that thought, is it an exchange of thought or is it that I am more fortunate than you? Do you see the difference between the belief system that I would incorporate and your society's beliefs?

"If I believe that you know more and believe that society also knows more, then there would be no difference. But, if I recognize I have choice and perceive your thoughts as an exchange, then I can make my own decision."

And so, you are then limited by your physical reality, or so it would seem.

"Yes."

It is possible to see it as an exchange and not an unfortunate circumstance. If there is no more change would it mean you have gone back to a bad life?

"No."

Perhaps in future you will adopt a clearer understanding of my statement. As I have mentioned before, if you view change as good, then is no change bad? When Christ came was it good? When Christ left was it bad? You have many different thoughts within and around you. Bring all your thoughts together as one force, as one element, and draw the energy from this whole thought. From there, you will become whole yourself.

Five fingers brought together is a fist. *(Seth demonstrated.)* There is power in bringing the individual fingers together. Each finger contains the same energy, but as a fist, the energy is focused and creates a force nonexistent than when the fingers are separate. Yet, the power of a fist is also limited. You cannot play the piano with a fist. Similarly, you have the capability to use all your thoughts in many ways, but the energy is stronger when all of your thoughts come together. Therefore, recognize that your thought system has more potential beyond what you are using it for now and in this you will discover a new sense of empowerment.

As you put together more pieces of the puzzle, you will experience a greater sense of accomplishment. Use your energy and thought system to benefit yourself and those around you. If I show you love, respect, and compassion, I can only hope that you will show the same to someone else and set them free.

It has been a complete and total picture of enjoyment to speak and exchange thoughts with you this evening.

"Thank you very much."

Be at peace with yourself and allow your system of thought to generate thought and that in itself is creation.

I felt unclear in completely understanding all of what Seth was saying.

I didn't stay long after the session as I had heard someone enter near the end, but Dale and I spoke briefly.

As we said our goodbyes, Dale was silent for a few seconds, and then said he was getting the message that we should pay attention and remember our dreams tonight.

I hoped I would have a good dream since over the last couple of weeks, I couldn't remember any of them.

I explained to Dale how my mind usually visualizes in picture form to assess what is happening. However, my problem seems to be in transposing the information from my mind to the page, or in verbalizing it.

I am very much a visual person, and as Seth spoke this evening, I felt myself drift off. As much as I tried to stay focused on everything he was saying, I faded in and out of the session numerous times, uncertain of whether I was falling asleep, just meditating, or whether my thoughts were being drawn into spirit. I find it difficult to clearly articulate my many thoughts, to know more about who I am and what I can create visually and materially.

Seth always left me with a need to know more about my inner self and I realize that eventually I will understand others more clearly. I had a feeling this evening that Seth handed me the key to open the door to my ideas and a new world of thinking. This was a revelation he did not verbalize through Dale but more through my own thought processes.

DREAMS

Thursday, June 4, 1998 - The weather had cooled down somewhat today but it was still pleasant. I arrived later than usual and the front door was closed. I walked in past Dale's bedroom just as he poked his head out and drowsily said he would soon be out to join me. Laura was in the kitchen and she kept me company until we were ready to start the session. Everyone at the house had gone to Maine last weekend except for Laura. I asked her what she had done while we were gone. She simply said she enjoyed spending the time on her own.

Dale joined us soon afterwards and as we prepared for tonight's session, I explained my dream from the night before.

If two minds think alike, how long would it take to change the world?

Dreams are a language for expressing what the soul sees and understands. The soul communicates through energy and light. The mind and its thoughts filter what is expressed through the soul and then manifest this expression into your physical reality. Your soul may desire physical freedom and express this desire in dreams where you may be either hiking in the wilderness or climbing a mountaintop while riding an elephant. You may be unable to decipher the meaning of this dream, but the elephant could represent the freedom of living on a mountain. The whole dream and its context are very important. To

113

analyze it, you must remove your emotions because your desires and emotions can block the clarity of the dream's message. You may believe that freedom comes with financial wealth and this belief may hinder your understanding of the dreams that actually express your desire for freedom.

To interpret your dreams, tap into what the soul has communicated through your thoughts and retrieve the appropriate message. To analyze your dreams, trust your 'self' and your intuition.

I began explaining my dream to Seth.

"I was in a home, sparsely furnished other than a corner area where three of us were silently working—a woman, a man and myself. After working for a while, the woman left the room and returned in tears and angry with me. She said I didn't pay enough attention to her, nor did I ever help her, and that things for her were difficult. I was surprised since her outburst was quite unexpected."

"I let her settle down and we continued on with our work. We had been each writing speeches to deliver to an audience. But when the time came for us to give our speeches, the other two went on stage and presented a lively and entertaining act advertising commercial products. Standing in the background and watching, I was impressed by the brilliance of their skits. I was also surprised because I thought we were supposed to write a speech that would reveal important news, which is what I had done. So I continued to go over the one that I had prepared."

"As the time came closer for me to speak, I realized that they were bringing a breakfast cereal on the stage and I sensed that this was what my speech was supposed to be about. I began to worry about how I was going to pull it off. I went on stage and began to greet the audience when I realized I had interrupted the woman who was introducing me. I let her finish and then someone from the audience bellowed, 'Hey, Hi! I just want to say hello to you.' I felt stuck and instead of doing the speech I prepared, I began to talk about the cereal. I was unprepared and didn't know what to say. I only heard myself mumble something and my dream ended."

Seth began his analysis.

Your dream is a reflection of your desire to be noticed as an individual who is intelligent and respected by others. The woman criticizing you is how you expect the public will perceive you. Preparing to speak before an audience, only to find that what you prepared is not what is expected, is a reflection of your fear that you will not be recognized for your capabilities. You were raised as a child with these thoughts.

The person from the audience who stood up and said "hello" is the part of you that feels at home sitting with the average people. Your disappointment with the speech shows your disappointment with your life up to this point. The three people at the table are three parts of your 'self' that have not been expressed yet. However, remembering and monitoring your dreams, represents your growing awareness and stronger control over different aspects of your life.

Does this make sense to you?

"Yes."

It made a lot of sense to me. I could relate to everything Seth said; it was a very familiar feeling. I feel I have a strong desire to express what I know but I always fall short just when I think I can do it. In the past couple of years, there have been a few occasions when the urge to express myself is very strong. An unknown energy will rise from deep within myself and it is then that I feel I'm right on the verge of being able to express myself, and I can then let go.

This soul, Dale Landry, is uncertain of whether he wants his dream expressed in the book, but I believe he has little to fear.

Dale didn't get a chance to reveal his dream to me before the session started, but Seth provided an analysis anyway.

There is a man in Dale's life, at a distance, who Dale rarely sees. We'll call him Tom. In life and in the dream, Tom is very masculine, but he has a sensitive side which Dale consciously knows about. Dale thinks it is unusual for Tom to appear in his dreams, but in the last two years, Tom has appeared in several of Dale's dreams and the dreams have always been significant.

In the dream from last night, Dale is aware of Tom's attraction to him and his desires for Dale's company. But when Dale goes to be with him,

Tom pulls away quickly and runs off. Later, Dale sees Tom and an unknown woman in a bar. Dale watches him from the other end of the bar. Then, both Dale and Tom are standing by a car. Dale watches as Tom has sex with a third man. The dream ends when Tom says to Dale, "He doesn't like it."

In his waking state Dale uses his senses and intuition to function, but in his dreams he uses his emotions. Dale only allows himself to feel in his dreams, a common occurrence among men. In the dream state, men are more likely to experience their female side because they feel less threatened.

As Seth was completing his analysis on Dale's dream, Dale quickly crossed his legs and folded his arms across his chest.

Seth sensed my reaction and asked the following question.

I wonder if he could close himself off anymore than what he just has?

Seth and I chuckled over Dale's discomfort.

It is rather interesting, don't you think, that a man like Dale can feel comfortable closing off to his emotions in the waking state?

Seth continued his analysis.

In his dream, even though Dale could not be with Tom, Dale felt a great deal of love towards him. Even when Dale is awake, he still has feelings of love for Tom. This is very unusual for Dale, but he has enjoyed the experience of these feelings.

The conflict for Dale is how can he feel love for a man he knows is a heterosexual and has expressed no interest in him? What Dale's dream also expresses is his capability to love and his pattern in love and relationships. In Dale's life, he has discovered that no matter who he is attracted to, they reject his attentions. This has been a pattern in Dale's life. Thus, in the dream, the man was attracted to Dale but ran from him, yet Dale continues to love him anyway. Dale is learning to love his patterns, to love each part of himself regardless of whether he gets what he wants in life. Even though one of the things he desires the most is a relationship, it continues to remain at arm's length. However, he still has love in his soul. The dream shows him that he is learning to go beyond a physical desire for love.

People are addicted to beliefs about love that are left unfulfilled. Going beyond your physical desire helps to release these feelings and beliefs of failure. You must learn to accept the rewards of who you are as an individual. Moving away from a limiting desire is also recognizing that you no longer are addicted to something that can destroy your mental, physical, emotional and spiritual health.

To interpret your dreams, you must write them down, even if the answers come only five years later. Each night you may dream the same thing, over and over again. It may be a different scenario every time, but the dreams will contain the same expression of your soul's desire and purpose. From the time you come into this physical reality until you leave, your soul keeps the same purpose; it never changes. It is as persistent as you are in your desire to live. One dream can be one frame of a long film, but each frame is as important as the next in providing a description of who you are.

In your youth, there are many dreams of monsters and other terrors that you do not understand in the morning. Often, these monsters are an aspect of your parents' unresolved fears that have been passed on to you as a child. In other words, your parents' anxieties are often expressed through you in your dream state.

Learning your soul's purpose and the reason for being here will not necessarily give you a sense of worth. It may actually make you feel insignificant. Dale feels that the more he hears and the more I speak, the less significant or important everything seems in life. However, that is only a reflection of his conscious beliefs and his physical desires. In essence, every soul desires the moment and in that moment there is nothingness. But from nothingness comes life and everything else.

As you grow and understand yourself, you will find that the more you know about your soul and its purpose, the more there is to know. As an entity unto yourself, you are still a part of the whole, the whole known as God and the whole of all individuals joined as one. Therefore, for all people living on this planet, there is not only your purpose that you must come to understand, but everyone else's. So when you have completed a piece of the puzzle, some part of your 'self', you must begin to put together another part. Each part of the puzzle is equally as important for each individual in order to complete the whole.

This is only a broad and general understanding of dreams. This book focuses on the creative expression of the self and it is from this perspective that I am looking at dreams.

Life is a game of illusions. What you believe you see in your waking state is often not a reality. As each moment moves towards another moment, you will understand that there is more to see through the soul and more to understand from your dreams.

In light of my departure from this session, I would simply like to say that, to live in the moment, is to die in the moment.

May God speed you to your destiny of the moment.

By the end of our session, only Dale and I were in the house so we decided to sit out in the yard and carry on the analysis of our dreams, their effects, how some appear as a premonition, and how others leave you confused upon wakening. There are also those dreams that wake you up in the middle of the night when you cannot remember anything except the frightening reality that you must wake up quickly to shake off the terrible sense of discomfort and fear.

TO DREAM
THE IMPOSSIBLE DREAM

*M*onday, *June 8, 1998 - Dale came out of the house as I arrived. No one else was home and we sat on the front porch to continue our discussion of dreams and the insights they provided about ourselves.*

Since returning from our trip to Maine, I have been feeling more tired than usual and spent much of my time sleeping. I considered the possibility that my body was processing the information I was receiving during these sessions with Seth. Dale, however, wasn't experiencing the same fatigue.

I will continue from where I left off at the end of our last session which was about dreaming. This soul, Dale Landry, that I am speaking through is reluctant to discuss his personal dreams because he is gay. In your society, this is not accepted, even though many believe that homosexuality has become more accepted. The only way society can change and accept people who are perceived differently is for everyone to divulge their innermost secrets. Many live with secrets whether they are dreams, thoughts, wishes or desires, and few rarely trust someone enough to reveal their true thoughts, feelings, or desires.

People fear that if they tell someone about their innermost secrets, it may be used against them. You and many others live in secrecy, never expressing or taking the time to understand yourself. From lifetime to lifetime, you scheme to get to the top, to find the perfect love, to have a successful career and to achieve popularity and independence. You never depend on anyone else because you fear they may turn on you, become envious or even destroy you. You have learned in your different lifetimes that your friends and family are the ones who can hurt you the most. It may seem obvious to you that the 'impossible' dreams are the ones that you know you can achieve, even if you never achieve them.

In any lifetime, the number of people who achieve success, inwardly or outwardly, is relatively low; only one or two per cent at most. So why dream the impossible dream? What will it take to give yourself permission to dream, or better yet still to desire and then express your dreams and innermost secrets?

For those who achieve material success, there is always the threat that someone will eventually take it away. There is a fear that government or society will bring them down. When you think of someone who is famous, you often believe that he or she lives an extraordinary life, you believe this person possesses many exceptional talents. But you are also talented and exceptional, so who judges your worth? You? God? Society? Religion? Family? To live in secrecy is to deny yourself an advantage. I am not telling you to reveal everything about yourself. I am saying you should know yourself enough to express who you are. Can you allow yourself to be different and show your fears, your ignorance and the human side of yourself? Can you allow yourself to feel compassion, sympathy and empathy? What will it take for you and others to achieve your innermost desires?

In your world, women more readily accept gayness, not because women have more compassion or empathy, but because they emotionally understand what it is like to have little power. Women understand what it is like to live in a patriarchal society that favours white heterosexual males. Heterosexual men fear homosexuals because of their own misguided desires for love, compassion and understanding. Homosexual men mirror the weaknesses of heterosexual men. They mirror what a heterosexual man will hide in order to be accepted by his peers.

This is a strong generalization but it is why homosexuality remains unacceptable? It is why homosexuals choose to live in large urban centres where they are more accepted and can live more openly. What I say is questionable, but anything you fear you will question, regardless of whether it is true or not. This is not a statement to encourage the liberation of gay men and women. It is a discussion about freeing the self. What you fear and deny in others is what you fear and deny in yourself.

I speak not as an authority but as one soul to another. Through many given lifetimes, you have all been persecuted, whether it was due to your skin colour, your gender, your affluence or your poverty. Yet, still, you carry from each lifetime the fear that you cannot speak out. Even being in a position of power limits your ability to speak out because you fear you will lose your power and will be forced to share it with others. These fears keep everyone chained together.

All people live in the same prison, only in separate cells. Thus, when everyone finds the means to help each other accomplish their desires, they will learn responsibility, commitment and all other things vital to having a rich and fulfilling life. To deny others help out of fear that they won't help you is to deny a part of your 'self'. You must move forward to achieve your dreams regardless of what others do. If you wait for others to make your dreams come true, to support you and to love you, it is too late. Begin now and eventually others will join you.

As Shakespeare wrote

"All the world is a stage,
And all the men and women merely players."

But to this I say, "All of the world is a stage and no one yet a player."

If your desire is to act, then act, without the expectation that you must be acknowledged as the best. If you want to sing, sing without the need for others to listen. If you want money, then work to make money without the fear that someone else may achieve greater wealth than you. Achieve your goals and enjoy your own success.

What is the purpose of your accomplishments if you don't enjoy them? Don't climb a mountain if your purpose is for others to envy you; climb the mountain because you want to get to the top and experience every step along the way. Climb because you want to know what the mountain is, see its beauty and learn its secrets. There are so many empty accomplishments in life, and many just wander through their desires, sometimes building, sometimes even growing, but without satisfaction. What is it that stops you from having that sense of accomplishment? Does your God tell you that life must always be empty and painful, or do you tell it to yourself?

If you make a wish, are you willing to make the wish come true? Some people live double lives and do not feel connected. Everyone and everything is disjointed and disconnected because so few are willing to make the effort to connect to those close to them. Few are willing to look at the solutions, and would rather focus on the problems.

It often seems that the world is ending due to disease, war and pollution. Who will take responsibility? Will the problem get so bad that you have no choice but to change? Who will pay for the change? If your governments are incapable of working efficiently, then why do so few work to change the government?

A small number of people have taken responsibility by changing their own lives and the lives of those around them, and as you become more committed to your own life, the changes will eventually transpire. For example, you may assume that love does not exist, but secretly you search for it endlessly and seek it daily. It seems to be everywhere in society but it is not there for you. Why does love constantly elude you? Do you ever ask yourself why you have no love? Do you know how to love another person and what is actually required? Can you be independent and at the same time love someone else? What are your motives for seeking love? Do you want love to be acceptance by your peers or do you just want to feel accepted? Can you feel love for yourself or do you deny yourself that precious commodity which is worth so much? Can you ever think back to a time when you felt love for yourself? If the answer is no to any of these questions, then there is work for you to do.

What is lacking in life is the understanding and the desire to know what you are about, where you want to go and what you really want to have. If you see that people around you are unfortunate and alone, this is because the world is a reflection of yourself.

The only way out of this dilemma is to challenge yourself. Create a world for yourself that is harmonious and spend time with people you like as well as those you don't. Both are important to understanding your true self.

Dale Landry should not fear his desire to love another man. This is a challenge people are dealing with in your physical reality where some are conscious of their desires and others are not. Throughout history homosexuals have been ridiculed and shamed. Today, homosexuality is still used to shame people into believing they are worth less. But are you worth less or are you worth more if you take on a greater challenge?

Your physical reality is a great challenge in itself. If people supported one another, imagine the obstacles society could overcome. When society accepts love among and between the sexes, it will be a more harmonious place to live.

I want to pass on a secret to those who feel hindered by their desire for a same sex relationship. People who negatively challenge you, who deny you the same freedom that they believe they have, who classify you as evil for being gay or thinking gay thoughts, have a secret desire to possess their own creativity and love of life. However, they do not allow themselves the same freedom. They want to destroy in others the very thing they do not allow themselves to have. People who live with the idea that their God despises anything they perceive to be different have a far greater challenge than those who desire to have love with a same sex partner.

This touching and heartfelt tribute by Seth to Dale was quite an emotional moment.

Overcome by the experience myself, I felt my own tears begin to surface as my dear friend was acknowledged with such love and respect.

I dedicate this chapter to this soul that I speak through, Dale Landry. For regardless of his past, his failings or shortcomings and disregarding that he may never find contentment, peace of mind or love, he has pursued with unimaginable passion a desire to find the true purpose and essence of what life is about. To this end, he has found what may not seem to be the perfect life, but he has given himself the permission to be imperfect, ignorant and to make mistakes. In so doing, Dale has come to a place of 'knowing'.

Hear the words I say. Love is there for the taking and if one desires to take it, he or she will see that it was already there before it was taken.

Until I shall be here in the moment again, may your God speed you towards the moment.

I discovered something about myself this evening that was never apparent before. I realized that I have a lot of dreams, aspirations and unspoken thoughts. With everything Seth spoke about in the session tonight, I found myself constantly asking why I had not undertaken many of the challenges that would have helped me to manifest my dreams? I became aware that no matter how attractive, intelligent, ugly, beautiful or stupid one is, he or she may not find the opportunity to invest in their dreams. I was saddened by this thought but still felt that, for me, opportunities to manifest my passions and desires were just beginning.

It is astounding the impact that words, support and permission can give to help one move forward with his or her life. I wasn't feeling so stuck now as I had when the sessions first started, and I wasn't sure exactly what it was that had changed, but I felt good about the changes nonetheless.

IMPERSONATIONS

Tuesday, June 9, 1998 - Dale was in a superb mood when I met him this evening. He told me how fabulous his whole day was. His mood was contagious and I soon found myself beginning to lighten up. Dale said he woke up this morning from a dream where wonderful music was playing in his head and asked if I had had the same experience. I did not, but it was amusing watching Dale enjoy himself, merrily dancing to the music he was listening to.

I, on the other hand, had arrived feeling as if I was coming down with a cold. I wasn't really sick, but felt I was probably undergoing further changes within myself while I sat in on and learned from these sessions.

If you could impersonate anyone you wanted, who would it be? I am not asking who would you like to be but who would you like to impersonate? There are many avenues to consider for these questions, and you should select your answer carefully.

Now, I shall talk about the differences between how most women and men would respond to this question.

To begin with, you may think that you have many responses to the questions I am asking, but in fact there are only a handful of individuals who people want to impersonate, such as Marilyn Monroe, Sophia Loren and Raquel Welch. Some women may choose Marilyn Monroe,

Raquel Welch or another modern-day personality because of an underlying desire to be adored by men and to gain men's love. Thus, it makes sense that most women would likely choose another woman, who is considered a sex object, to impersonate.

Women do not typically choose to impersonate men of perceived power, such as the United States President, because women traditionally desire love as opposed to power. I am not stating that women want to be sex objects or that women who desire strength can't find love. But women generally deal with things from an emotional level and, in this regard, have a stronger desire for love. In some ways, it is a woman's most important desire.

You may find it amusing to learn that, if given the opportunity, men would also choose to impersonate a woman. Like women, most men would choose a youthful Marilyn Monroe, Sophia Loren or Raquel Welch, but for a different reason.

Many men believe that in being an object of desire, they could have as much sex as they wanted with as little effort as possible. There is a common belief among men that women do not work at having sex. At the same time, many relatively effortless sexual encounters lead men to feel loved. Thus, men feel love through sex, and in turn women feel love through desire.

Men and women, however, fail to recognize how each other thinks. This lack of understanding is often the cause of the communication break down between both sexes. It is like two trains travelling side by side on opposite tracks. From one train you can view the other, but rarely, if at all, will the two meet unless they collide head-on.

Women believe that men are incapable of feeling emotion and are resentful that men do not deal with the emotional turmoil they sometimes experience. Alternatively, men believe that women are absorbed in their emotions and resent that women do not acknowledge a male's feelings. Women need to understand that men do experience emotion and also understand how and why they feel the way that they do.

Men feel the most intense emotions during a sexual encounter. It is at this point that men's emotions peak and they can connect with the outside world. Whether it is sex with a woman or another man, a sexual encounter allows men to communicate and understand their surroundings in ways they do not when they are not having sex.

Does this mean that men experience intense emotions infrequently - maybe ten percent of the time? Yes. How often do women know what men are feeling? About ten percent of the time, usually during sex.

Having sex allows men and women to experience a heightened awareness, a connection to the soul's energy and light. Do not fear having sex to experience this heightened state. The true fear of sex often comes from society and religion which propels the belief that you will be punished for having it. After sex some men desire a cigarette, but the cigarette is not the desire, the calming effect it produces is what men desire. Once calm, men can consider who they truly are and what they experienced emotionally during sex. Women, on the other hand, want to be loved and nurtured after sex because the act has heightened their awareness of their purpose to be desired.

In homosexual relationships, both gay men and gay women experience relative extremes in their response to sex. Gay men may desire to leave after sex because, subconsciously, they do not feel secure in their emotional state and cannot balance their energy after the sexual act. A conscious awareness of this insecurity and imbalance can allow a gay man to overcome this sense of 'fight or flight'. Lesbians on the other hand tend to over-nurture one another. Again, it is important that there is a conscious awareness of how to balance the situation.

It is believed that after sex, men experience a despondency and woman desire more closeness. The difficulty arises in women's dependence and men's irresponsibility. If men were responsible, they would ensure that women felt nurtured, and if women were independent, they would not feel the need for more attention.

There is a universal law that if you force someone or something in one direction, there is an equal force pushing back. When each of you learn to draw back, you will learn to be responsible and hold your own and you will discover that others are more willing to give. But if you are constantly asking or demanding, you will encounter the same resistance.

For centuries, men have been conditioned to withhold their emotions, not knowing how to express their feelings. Women, on the other hand, have been taught to express their emotions unconditionally. The scales are not balanced, however, the solution is simple. Be yourself and achieve independence, and emotional openness will follow.

During sex, it is important that women are open and receptive to what is being given emotionally. If nothing is given, then she must evaluate if she has chosen the right relationship, regardless of whether there are children with this man. The minute she questions whether she has made the right choice is the moment the man begins to change and respond to her. She does not have to explain her thoughts for that will only push him farther away.

Men who desire a fulfilling relationship must consider their partner and ensure she is satisfied and enjoying their sexual relationship. He must be willing to change to ensure she changes also. The purpose of sex is not just the physical pleasure, but to enjoy the energy that flows between two people who truly care about each other.

People believe that there are many rules to love, but love has no absolutes. You can love a friend, man or woman, as deeply as you love your partner, even though society believes this is unhealthy or wrong.

People pray to God, yet do not feel love when they pray. Have you considered why you are not feeling the love of your all-loving God? Through the centuries and through the lifetimes, you have been taught that God is loving but will punish you if you do something wrong. Your fear of this punishment prevents you from feeling God's love. So how can you love what you fear? How can you find forgiveness and openly love a God you are frightened of?

The next time you pray, ask God to remove the obstacles that keep you from feeling His or Her love, and the love of the many souls in your physical life and beyond.

Recently, your world was stunned by the death of a princess, Lady Diana. There was a great deal of sadness about how someone so beautiful and young could have been taken so quickly. But people felt not only the loss of the woman, but also of the unconditional love she gave to the world. As a society, you strive to find unconditional love, but also find it difficult to give this love in return. Lady Diana is an example of how one can unconditionally love your neighbour regardless of race, colour, faith or position in life.

Set an example for those around you and love without expectations that they must love you back. There is a common belief that you cannot love someone who does not love you in return. But how can you not love a person regardless of whether you want to possess them? Does your God stop loving you because you cannot love Him or Her as much as He or She loves you?

Approach life from the perspective that you will live it to the fullest and embrace whatever it has to offer you, regardless of the pain and difficulties you encounter. To understand your life, you must eliminate your expectations of what you believe you have to achieve. If you operate from this perspective, there are no disappointments, and every encounter and experience is a joy to live through. Even if you who have lost a loved one, know that love does not die and that to have loved someone in itself is an experience to be treasured and thankful for.

Feeling angry about your life and feeling that it is unfair, only keeps you closed off to the incredible possibilities. Embrace your shortcomings and eventually you will understand that life in your physical world is never unfair. Holding onto the idea that life is unfair is just an illusion. Sooner or later, the light within you will move from your physical body to seek freedom as freedom is a part of who you will always be. In the end, strive not to find freedom but to find purpose, because with purpose comes freedom.

In life, do look not for love, but rather, to be 'love'. When you feel lost and confused along your pathway, accept it as a part of the journey and enjoy the experience of feeling confused and uncertain.

When it comes time for you to leave this physical world, do not regret the way you have lived your life. Look back and say, I lived it all.

I am unsure if you will truly understand what has been said over these past two sessions. It is quite a departure from what I have said in the rest of the book, but it is important and relevant since it deals with self-expression. Often, people try to express themselves through love, sex, people they meet, their life purpose and everything else that they can be. Religion is also an expression of the self, and whatever religion you choose is an aspect of your own thoughts and its expression.

Seth continued on a personal note.

This soul, Dale Landry, wanted to know the meaning of the music in the dream he awoke to this morning. He found it exciting and it gave him a sense of well being. Simply put, the music was symbolic of his life at that moment. This music was playing his song and it reflected how nicely things are going; he's in the groove of things so to speak.

Seth then asked me if I had any questions, but I did not.

May God speed you towards the moment and may the bus get you there on time.

"Thank you."

I was speechless by the time Seth had finished tonight. It was another hard hitting session with provoking thoughts and not enough solutions to the many questions which passed through my mind. It was interesting to discover so much about how men approach life and their perceptions of what they believe is important in comparison to my own. I always believed from the time I was young that many men, and some women, were very happy, and that I was one of the few unfortunate ones left to rot away. Now that I hear and see all that is being said in these sessions, I feel so stupid and pathetic that I could have been so naive to foolishly believe that I was more unfortunate than other people. Information, knowledge and wisdom can truly set one free.

SESSION 18

CHANGING THE WORLD

Wednesday, June 10, 1998 - This evening Sarah was alone in the kitchen. Dale was engaged in a phone conversation in the basement, so Sarah and I discussed our day's activities.

I made my way downstairs to see Dale who was still on the phone and let him know I was ready.

This week we were taking it much easier. The sessions were starting a little later than usual, and we were spending more time talking to each other and the others who were at home or dropping by. I knew the sessions were winding down and it was reflected by the more quiet and passive mood I was experiencing. I sensed the book was coming to a close, and the joy and anticipation I always felt during Seth's dictation was changing to a feeling of loss.

Brilliant ideas have been formulated with each moment in time and whether people accept these ideas or not, they will eventually come back once again. There have been many thoughts on how to change your life and how to change the world, but you cannot change one without the other. For instance, as you change, others around you will also change. The changes may seem subtle and sometimes unapparent, but they do occur.

To create change, you must understand the direction and purpose of the change. A slim man may want to change his body to become more

131

muscular. But first he must recognize that change is possible, and then he must desire it.

To create physical change requires time, effort and most importantly, persistence. You should be conscious of your objectives at all times, whether you are doing inner work or not. Eventually, if your mind persists in holding true to your goals, the work can begin.

There is a common belief that only people who hold positions of power can make great changes to effect issues such as poverty, homelessness and other complex problems. All changes begin at 'home', and home is where the heart resides, for the heart represents the home. Therefore, to create a peaceful world you need to create a peaceful life for yourself. You need to recognize the home. To save another person, you must first learn to save yourself.

The widely-held belief that your physical world will end symbolizes a subconscious desire to end your inner work and the pain, and reflects a desire to return 'home' to spirit or the metaphysical reality. Your hope in this world is to have purpose and it is at home, in spirit, where there would no longer be emptiness or pain. Peace would prevail, but beyond this is the reality that many worlds of consciousness exist. This, however, may be difficult to conceive for fear that there will be endless pain.

To know that your inner work is an unending challenge will help you manifest what you desire and propel you to move on to your next goal. With work comes responsibility, with responsibility comes freedom, and with freedom comes a sense of purpose, peace and contentment. It is impossible to have one without the other. To desire love is to work for it, become independent of it, and discover how to obtain it. Love must be able to move freely within yourself and must have the freedom to come and go like the wind blows through the trees. Even when the wind has disappeared and the trees are calm and silent, it will still loom close in the background. Love may appear to be absent, but like the wind, it will always exist. People believe that when they die they will cease. But they will always be alive, just in a different way than what they perceive in this moment.

As you decide to change inwardly, you will find your world outside also changing. As you become more emotionally independent, those around you will also become more independent. Your inner self reflects your reality. If you are filled with feelings of emptiness, pain and anger, your outside world will also be filled with the same despair. When you find harmony and peace within, you will discover harmony and peace in the world around you.

When you are capable of loving yourself, others will love you too. But if you do not love yourself, you cannot ask someone else for it. If you become entangled in a web of deceit and pretend to love yourself, then you will draw in someone who will also pretend to love you. Changing your beliefs will free you from the web you create and will bring about freedom.

I offer you the following story.

One day two farmers who lived next to each other began to argue about who had more. The first farmer believed that, because his wife and children were more beautiful than the second farmer's, he had more. But the second farmer believed he had even more because, not only were his wife and his children beautiful, they were also intelligent. The two men continued to argue until their wives came along and overheard them. The women looked at each other and laughed for they knew that in many ways both men lived in poverty. Neither man could tell his wife and children how beautiful they were and how much they enjoyed them. And, not realizing their errs, each man would argue over who had the best family.

Like these two farmers, people will argue with anyone who says their life is not perfect, but when they are alone and filled with a sense of sadness, they will not admit to it. You will find strength to change when you admit to your weaknesses. By recognizing your limitations, you can begin to find a solution. To change the world, you must first change yourself. Only then will you be able to admit to your imperfections and accept others who need your help. Your physical reality may seem complicated and unchangeable. But it is only this way if you believe it to be. You can dream of a world in which everyone lives in harmony, or you can make it a reality.

Most material achievements require effort. You can't buy a house unless you work and save money. But love, peace and harmony also require work, even if we hold onto the false assumption that God can provide these rewards to those He or She favours. Remember, to live with beauty and intelligence is the same as living with pain and emptiness, and this is the same for one who is ugly and stupid.

When you judge others and believe someone else is more fortunate or less fortunate than yourself, you judge both yourself and your beliefs. How you judge another person and place them into a category is a reflection of how you categorize yourself and your limitations.

People who have achieved a perceived high social status may consider themselves to be more productive than those who have not had similar successes. But your social status is not a reflection of your true worth or productivity.

You may want to belong to groups considered successful in society, such as doctors, teachers or lawyers. But to belong to such a group offers only a perception that you have achieved a high social status and purpose in your life. When you reach spirit, the metaphysical reality, will you still believe that these professional titles are valuable, or will you be a soul just like all the others?

To overcome the restraints of your world, reject the notion that your profession is a symbol of your value and spiritual achievements. Whether you are a national leader or a store clerk, you are first and foremost a human being with desires and needs like everyone else. Denying this will only create more emptiness. It is a false illusion that people in powerful positions have different needs or desires than those with fewer professional accomplishments. For everyone in your physical reality there is pain, emptiness and loneliness, but there is also love, justice, balance and harmony.

To cleanse yourself of the pain is not to lose the pain itself, but to acquire a new perception of it. Feeling love is only a different way of looking at the pain. To live a full life is another way of looking at death, for in all things there is only one thought, each contributing to the cumulative value of the total thought. Each of you are an intricate part of that thought.

I heard Rick come home during the session but didn't see him until it was over. Corinne showed up shortly after Rick, and Sarah, Rick and Corinne decided to see a movie, The Horse Whisperer. *I stayed awhile longer with Dale and then left for the evening.*

On my way home, I found myself reflecting on all of the sessions we had covered so far, and I couldn't help but wonder what the full impact would be in my years to come. A part of what I felt for Seth was that I had found my soulmate; someone who loved and supported me unconditionally, with no strings attached, and who had all of my best interests at heart. Now, in a matter of days, perhaps another week, the sessions would end and I couldn't help but feel death as my companion as I slowly drove home.

*S*ESSION **19**

THE WANDERER

*Sunday, June 14, 1998 - With the sessions almost completed, we
decided to hold a session on a Sunday, not our usual day. I worked
on transcribing the book during the early part of the afternoon and
arrived at Dale's just before 5 p.m.*

*Unexpected visitors arrived to see Dale, so again, our session was
delayed. Sarah was in the backyard and we kept each other company
on this sunny afternoon until Dale was ready. Rick soon joined us and
eventually Dale was free to join us all as well.*

*After Sarah and Rick left, instead of starting our session right away,
Dale treated me to a meal at a nearby restaurant.*

*I couldn't help but wonder if this was a part of Dale's pattern to never
start on time. I do not really know the reason for his always being late.*

For many people, their purpose is to continually wander and search
for information as they travel through life's experiences. I shall now
discuss what is important to you and to this soul, Dale Landry, that I
speak through.

People question the relevance of their existence, their different
thoughts, why they repeat limiting patterns, and why they never learn
or understand their limitations.

What is the most important question you could ask yourself in this moment of existence, Christine?

"Why am I here?"

Yes. Also, what is my purpose and can I ever achieve anything worthwhile? Will I be recognized and accepted? Will I find value and contentment? Will I find love? It is true that for even the one who wanders through life, he or she desires a partnership of value.

Each person's purpose has the same ring of truth. You may decide to exist on this physical plane and become a Doctor of Philosophy, a lawyer or a street person. Each of these people has something in common, experiencing life to the fullest in the situation they choose to exist. Life experience provides knowledge which is retained when you travel into spirit, and as you travel, there is no time. But there is the belief and expectation that travel takes time. However, as you travel, time does not exist; time is included in the travel.

The knowledge gained from travelling in and out of your physical existence creates a road map for you in spirit and beyond. This map is an indicator of whether your tank is half-full or empty. Some may believe that the tank must be full in order to make the journey, where others may feel the tank is always full, even if it's empty.

What you achieve in this physical reality is not important. What is of true value is experience, good or bad, painful or loving, compassionate or cold. Your experiences help you to have a richer, fuller, more contented life. But in and of itself, this does not give you greater importance or more status as many of you would like to believe.

When you know your purpose you can experience your life for what it is, not what you expect it to be. Many people see life as a maze, with many twists and turns, dead ends and with no beginning or end. But there is a beginning and an end, and the end is a new beginning. Understand the confusion by accepting where you are in life at any given point. In old age, you may understand that there is no reward for simply getting there. To regard youth as the only special time is to believe that pain is everlasting.

To accept where you are in the moment helps you to find balance and harmony. Through balance and harmony you will learn to discover the moment. It is believed in your society that God will protect the weak, the confused, the pained and the unloved, and will lift them out of their distress. But why should God lift you out of your pain and distress if you have chosen to stay in it? You are a part of God and you can choose how to live your life and get out of your pain.

You have the choice to find self-expression and creativity. God has given you that opportunity and will not take it away. Asking for guidance, insight and to be lifted from the pain and confusion of every day living is the choice to have greater understanding and peace of mind. Choose a new path to create a sense of freedom and independence. To believe that God must relieve you of your pain is to believe that God will not help you. To believe that love exists is also to believe that love does not exist. To find love, you must understand the absence of love. You will find your answers when you understand the presence and absence of pain, suffering and love.

Your purpose is locked within your own thought process and feelings. Men may discover their direction more easily than women, but men may also make bad choices that have nothing to do with their true purpose. They make choices based on monetary reward and the idea that money will come easily.

There is a belief, especially in North America, that those who have physical beauty can achieve much more with little effort. But having a backyard does not always mean you will have a flourishing garden. A garden requires work, and it is an illusion that those who are exceptionally attractive are exempt from work, trouble and pain. There is also a common belief that those who are seen as unattractive are lonely and unloved. But those who are physically beautiful who read these words will smile and understand that they, too, are lonely. If you are attractive, people usually desire your company for how you look, not for who you are. Those who are attractive can mask their ugliness and inability to feel content. They have expectations others cannot possibly meet. So which is worse, to be beautiful or to be ugly? Maybe those who lie in the middle of this equation are the ones who feel true contentment. However, they may also feel that they are too mundane to achieve much in life; they may feel that they are only half of what they could be.

There are many physically attractive people who want to believe that they can use their beauty for external gain and accept what others project onto them. But deep within, their soul cries out in pain. You can believe the illusions of beauty, but it is those individuals who find a sense of self and accept their shortcomings, beautiful or ugly, who settle for less and will end up with more. It is not the most money or status that these people will receive, but a greater understanding of life and its imperfections.

To unravel your soul's outward purpose is to also accept the idea that you may never discover it. But in that acceptance, you will realize your suffering because you will not understand your purpose. However, by giving yourself the permission to fail, you will succeed and be humbled by your simple existence. Through an inability to perfect yourself outwardly you will discover the perfection that lies within. Everything around you, people or otherwise, is a mirror of the inner part of yourself that you have not yet seen. But as you learn to listen and see what you don't have emotionally, you will uncover where you want to be mentally, and discover it was always there to begin with.

To believe that people who are homeless, or mentally or physically challenged are less fortunate is to deny that you are also faced with similar challenges. An emotional challenge can be as difficult to deal with as a physical challenge; both are equally painful and debilitating.

You will grow inwardly when you accept people who are believed to be less fortunate, because what you do unto others will be done unto you. Loving unconditionally will allow others to love you back. Your world does not want to let go of the beliefs that hinder its progress. But to accomplish change, you must accept what you have denied, face the problem and deal with the ailments that stop you from moving forward.

Assassinating Martin Luther King did not stop the African American movement, rather, it assisted them to know their enemy. John F. Kennedy Jr. and Robert Kennedy were not the enemies, but because of their good intent, they were an impediment to those with alternative ideals.

Your world destroys people who do not adopt a common belief system. So why does society adopt such rigid ideals and absolute beliefs about life? Is there no room for individuality? You have strength when you can allow others to be different. If you try to change others, you will create adverse change in yourself. To respect others and their opinions costs you nothing. And to rely on others does not mean you are weak, it only means that you are open and receptive.

In the era known as the sixties, there was an expression heralded by the masses, "Make love, not war." Throughout the different lifetimes you have existed, there has been a constant desire to have love, not war. But when you are unable to make others love you, you create war in anger.

Justice is not the justice you have been taught. Justice results when you can understand someone else, see what they have done to hurt themselves or others, and know that you could easily do the same. Through each lifetime, each soul carries with themselves their own sense of justice. Whatever that soul does to hinder or hurt it, will create its own justice, a personal 'rule of law'. That is not God's punishment, it is a part of you that is already God.

Your justice system, at this moment, no longer operates efficiently and it is unable to correct the abuse inflicted upon it. In due course, it too will crumble and be replaced by a new system. This new system will be more lenient and offer more freedom, but will also require more individual responsibility. At this time, neither the justice system nor the government is run by the people, and as a result the people believe that someone else should run their society and determine its rules and its structure. When everyone decides together that they want change for the better, there shall be change enjoyed by all. This is the essence of Rousseau's *The Social Contract*.

I am not saying that your current government or justice system is wrong or corrupt. Most people are uninterested in how these systems operate, and this is the reason why they no longer work to their optimum. If you neglect your health, over time, your health will fail. The same goes for society.

To discover yourself, ask the questions, "Who am I? What do I want? Where am I going?" It does not matter when you ask these questions, but once you start, do not end there because the answers will change as you begin to change.

Once again, may God speed you towards the moment.

When the session finished, Dale and I talked about the changes that were occurring in his life.

In a separate discussion with Seth, he said to me, "It might be worthwhile to mention that there is a lot of work already transpiring for another book to be written. This new book will overlap the work on the one you are doing now. But the sessions in the next book will take on a much different flavour. Everything in life overlaps, and people often don't see it."

With talk of another book coming about, I couldn't help but wonder who Dale would be channelling and whether or not I would be invited to participate. As much as I hated to see things end with Seth, a new interest was ignited with the prospect of doing more of this type of work. I could only hope that my ugliness would work as a benefit in the next book also.

Once again, Dale and I joined the group that had formed in the backyard. By now Laura, and Dale's friends, Corinne and Rosaria, had shown up. I stayed on until later into the evening.

EXPERIMENTING WITH CHANGE
(THE CONCLUSION)

*M*onday, June 15, 1998 - This was to be our last session for the
book. I called Dale earlier in the day as I knew I would be a little
late this evening. Even though it was our last session, it was my first
time at really being late, not that I would have felt missed.

*Throughout my day, I was constantly being reminded of the noise that
one encounters, and today I was particularly sensitive to it. At every
turn, I was contending with the battering of noise in my eardrums;
which was annoying to say the least.*

*When I arrived at Dale's place, it continued, and I was quite aware
of the neighbourhood sounds; dogs barking, a train passing in the
distance and cars travelling back and forth. It had become so
overwhelming that I mentioned it to Dale and wasn't surprised to learn
that he was experiencing the same sensation. Exactly what it all meant,
I wasn't sure.*

As our session started this evening, the noise continued.

Wouldn't it be wonderful if you could put silence on a page instead
of words. Experimenting with a book of empty pages to symbolize an
author's silence would allow readers to also sense the solitude.

Every day you experiment, whether it is with new food or relating to
different types of people. To experiment with your emotions and to

express your love to a friend or family member may be a risk you do not want to endure. But in each experiment is the possibility of a reaction and a willingness to risk failure or rejection. Two worlds that collide may bring about great destruction, but they may also bring about a new world, one that is more harmonious than the original two.

Thirty or forty years ago, people experimented with new ideas about religion, home life and personal desires. A few years later, the outcome of these experiments was a revolution of change when individuals started taking responsibility for their own direction, their own beliefs and their own desires.

People feel a constant need to be loved, noticed, wanted, accepted, desired—even lusted after. These desires are instinctual, but society believes it is wrong to have such desires. Despite these beliefs, it is more important to simply know thyself. As your personal revolution continues, and as people change and create new ways of thinking, there is a stronger desire for new ideas, new thoughts and new ways to control the fear that comes with change. To deny that there is a revolution of change is to deny the obvious. In the last few decades, many transformations have taken place and it will not stop now. You have new ways to communicate, to understand and to develop. Many more changes are in store for all that will bring everyone closer together, but may also divide those who fear it.

As Robert Frost once wrote,

> Two roads diverged in the woods, and I -
> I took the one less travelled by,
> And that has made all the difference.

This was a short session, but it was only a prelude of the work ahead to complete the book. There was still a great deal left to do.

My evenings with Seth and Dale over these past few weeks were so enriching and fulfilling that I wanted them to continue.

I feel the need here to give some deep explanation of what working on this book has meant. A year or two before, when Dale asked if I was interested in doing personal growth classes with him, I was reluctant, but still, never so certain about something I wanted so much in my whole life. The reluctance was only monetary, but short lived when I weighed the possibilities of what I would get out of these classes. Now as I sit here, finishing this book with Dale, my initial intuition and impulse couldn't have been more correct. Working with Dale was the best choice I had ever made and the internal rewards keep returning, over and over, as I move through each week, each month, and beyond.

My personal growth work has helped me to see that there is so much more to life than having a 'loving' relationship, a house with the proverbial 'white picket fence', and an envied career with great financial returns. In my wildest dreams, I had never expected the happiness I would feel as I participated in something that seemed both so normal, yet so very unusual. I would never have thought that a different kind of love could take the place of a physical love and marriage.

Perhaps I should say here to each of you, expect the unexpected when you make the choice to work towards inner growth. It will come to you in ways you least expect.

TO CONTACT THE AUTHOR

Dear Reader, Seminar Coordinator or Meeting Planner:

Both the publisher and author want to know how you enjoyed *Seth: Creative Expression*. Please note that not every response can be answered. To provide comments, write to the address shown below.

To help ensure a reply, please enclose a self-addressed, stamped envelope or international postal reply coupon.

Dale Landry has been working and developing psychically as a trance channeller since 1983. He has been interviewed on Canada's *The Dini Petty Show*, Toronto's *640 AM*, national talk show *Jane Hawtin* as well as numerous other radio and television programs. Mr. Landry is available for events, seminars and workshops. For more information, please write, phone or fax:

Hushion House Publishing Limited
36 Northline Road
Toronto, Ontario
Canada M4B 3E2

Phone: 1-800-387-0141 **Ontario/Quebec**

1-800-387-0172 **All other provinces**

Fax: (416) 285-1777